AGS® *Reading Skills for Life*

Level A

AGS®

American Guidance Service, Inc.
Circle Pines, Minnesota 55014-1796
1-800-328-2560

D1088202

Content Reviewers

The publisher wishes to thank the following educators for their helpful guidance and review during the development process for *Reading Skills for Life*. Their assistance has been invaluable.

Jack Cassidy, Ph.D.
Professor of Education
Texas A&M University
Corpus Christi, Texas

James Johnston
Reading Specialist
Portsmouth High School
Portsmouth, New Hampshire

Alva Webb Jones, Ed.S.
Special Education Consultant
Richmond County Board of Education
Augusta, Georgia

Robin Pence
Reading Specialist
Clay High School
Clay County Schools
Green Cove Springs, FL

Ted Stuff
School Psychologist
Special Education Department Chair
McLaughlin High School
Anchorage, Alaska

Development and editorial services provided by Straight Line Editorial Development, Inc.

Photo and Illustration Credits

Page 4, Jeff Greenberg/PhotoEdit; pp. 6, 55, David Young-Wolff/PhotoEdit; pp. 9, 36 (left), 37, 43, 48, 67, 101, 106, 129, 134, Franklin Haws; pp. 13, 18, 25, 30, 70, 76, 125, 146, 152, 158, 164, Jean Schalk; p. 36 (right), Michelle Bridwell/PhotoEdit; p. 54 (top), Michael Newman/PhotoEdit; p. 54 (bottom), Tony Freeman/PhotoEdit; p. 82, Las Vegas Sun; p. 83, Dan Wylde; pp. 88, 89, 94, 95, Ave Green; p. 112 (left), Reuters/CORBIS-Bettmann; p. 112 (right), ©Bettmann/CORBIS; p. 171, Mary Steinbacher/PhotoEdit

Publisher's Project Staff

Director, Product Development: Karen Dahlen; Associate Director, Product Development: Teri Mathews; Editors: Maureen Meyer, Jody Peterson; Development Assistant: Bev Johnson; Designer and Cover Illustrator: Denise Bunkert; Design Manager: Nancy Condon; Desktop Publishing Specialist: Linda Peterson; Desktop Publishing Manager: Lisa Beller; Purchasing Agent: Mary Kaye Kuzma; Executive Director of Marketing: Matt Keller; Marketing Manager: Brian Holl

Printed in the United States of America

ISBN 0-7854-2637-X

Product Number 91700

A 0 9 8 7 6 5 4

CONTENTS

◆ Welcome!

Reading is like anything else that matters. In order to be good at it, you have to practice.

Here is how *Reading Skills for Life* will help you become a better reader:

▶ **You will learn the sounds that letters stand for.** Knowing the sounds letters stand for lets you figure out new words by sounding them out.

▶ **You will get to know important words by sight.** Some words can't be sounded out. You just have to remember the way they look. Knowing lots of words by sight is one big key to reading.

▶ **You will know how words can change.** This book will help you see how words change, and what the changes mean.

▶ **You will read better by reading more.** You will read stories about characters who face real-life problems and find solutions. You will also learn some facts about the real world. (Some of these may surprise you!) And you will read about some real people who have done amazing things.

▶ **You will learn about yourself.** Your ideas are important! This book will help you think about what you read. What **you** think about what you read matters. This book gives you plenty of chances to "be the judge."

With a little practice, you'll be reading like a pro in no time! So start reading!

◆ The Five Steps to Learning a Word

1. **Read the word.** Notice its shape. Is it long or short? What letters does it begin with? Does it look like other words you know?

2. **Say the word.** What sounds does it have? Which letters stand for those sounds?

3. **Write the word.** Get a feel for the word by writing it down.

4. **Add the word to your Word Bank.** You will find a Word Bank in the back of this book. It has space for you to write the new words you learn. Your Word Bank lets you keep track of all the words you are learning.

5. **Practice reading the word.** Read the word again and again until you know it.

◈ Tips for Reading Longer Words

Short words are usually simple to read. It's easy to get stumped when you come to longer words. Here are some tips that can help:

▶ **Look for word parts you know.** Is the word made up of a smaller word you know, plus an ending?

▶ **Look for letter patterns you know.** If you know one pattern of letters, like the **ain** in **main,** use it when you come to other words. Knowing **main** can help you read lots of words you may not know, such as **pain, train, stained,** and **raining.**

▶ **Break the word into parts.** Is the word made up of two smaller words that have been put together?

▶ **Look for syllables.** The vowels in a word are a clue to how many syllables it has.

▶ **Think about the sounds the letters stand for.** Look at the letters in the word. What sounds do the letters stand for? Blend all the sounds together to read the word.

◆ Using Context Clues

Sometimes the other words in a sentence give you clues to a word's meaning. Here's an example:

> The **trunk** is locked, and Jim has the car keys.

What does **trunk** mean in this sentence?

    a. the back part of a car

    b. an elephant's nose

    c. a big box for clothes

The words **locked** and **car keys** are context clues. They help you see that here, **trunk** means "the back part of a car."

Look for context clues when you read. You can find them everywhere!

REMEMBER . . .
If you try one tip for reading a word and it doesn't work, try something else. If all else fails, use a dictionary. Or ask a friend for help.

CHAPTER 1

Letters and Sounds

◆ **Directions:** The letters **a, e, i, o,** and **u** are vowels. Read these words. Circle the vowels.

a   e   i   o   u

1. j(a)b   2. m(e)t   3. d(i)d   4. n(o)d   5. c(u)t

> **TIP:** The words **jab, met, did, nod,** and **cut** all have a short vowel sound. They have the consonant-vowel-consonant pattern. Another way to say consonant-vowel-consonant is CVC.

◆ **Directions:** If you can read **jab,** you can read lots of words that end in **ab**. Read these words. Write them on the lines.

6. jab _Jab_   8. tab _tab_

7. nab _nab_   9. grab _grab_

◆ **Directions:** If you can read **did,** you can read lots of words that end in **id**. Read these words. Write them on the lines.

10. did _did_   12. skid _skid_

11. kid _kid_   13. lid _lid_

◆ **Directions:** Write the letters on the lines. See how many words you can make.

| j | f | r | b | h | gl | br | c | d | t |

14. _c_ an   22. _r_ ob

15. _t_ an   23. _gl_ ob

16. _r_ an   24. _b_ ob

17. _f_ an   25. _f_ ob

18. _r_ im   26. _c_ ut

19. _t_ im   27. _b_ ut

20. _j_ im   28. _h_ ut

21. _br_ im   29. ____ ut

Story Words

◆ **Directions:** Read each word to yourself. Then say the word out loud. Write the word on the line. Check the box after each step.

30. new   Read ☑ Say ☑ Write ☑   *new*

31. sound   Read ☑ Say ☑ Write ☑   *sound*

32. only (on | ly)   Read ☑ Say ☑ Write ☑   *only*

33. remember   Read ☑ Say ☑ Write ☑   *remember*
    (re | mem | ber)

34. plastic (plas | tic)   Read ☑ Say ☑ Write ☑   *plastic*

35. pocket (pock | et)   Read ☑ Say ☑ Write ☑   *pocket*

More Word Work

◆ **Directions:** You can add **s** to many words. Add **s** to make a word tell about more than one thing, or to make it tell about something going on now. Add **s** to each word.

Example: lid   lid + s = lids

36. kid   *kid*   + *s* = *kids*
37. swim   *swim*   + *s* = *swims*
38. blob   *blob*   + *s* = *blobs*
39. slob   *slob*   + *s* = *slobs*
40. shut   *shut*   + *s* = *shuts*

> **TIP:** For words that end in **x, ch, sh,** or **s,** add **es** instead of **s.**

◆ **Directions:** Add **es** to each word.

Example: dress   dress + es = dresses

41. wish   *wish*   + *es* = *wishes*
42. toss   *toss*   + *es* = *tosses*
43. miss   *miss*   + *es* = *misses*
44. box   *box*   + *es* = *boxes*
45. ranch *ranch* + *es* = *ranches*

Use What You Know

It is a hot, hot day. What can two pals find to do on a hot day? Write what you think on the lines below. Then read on to find out what Tim and Bob do.

The two pals can go swimming or set up a lemonade stand and sell lemonade.

THE DIVE GAME

"Tim! How long can this day get? It is way hot!" Bob picks up an ice cube and sets it on his skin. I pick up an ice cube and flip it at him. Bob asks, "Is our only plan to sit and flip ice cubes all day? How about a swim?"

"That sounds fine—the part about a swim, Bob. Or we could go fish over by Red Rocks. It may be a way to tune up our new **rods**."

Bob tosses the ice cube at me. It skids on my skin and slides down my spine. He nods a yes and prods my leg. "What about a dive game off the rocks?"

I jab him back. "OK, kid, I bet I can dive all the way down this time."

"Get out! You can not, you blob!" Bob yells.

I yell back, "Yes, I can, you slob!"

Bob and I grab our swim things and our bikes. We go to skid out of there fast. Only then do I remember what I have to do first. I have to pick up a ring for my mom. "Bob, I have to go by that shop, the Stone Hut. Remember? I have to pick up a ring for my mom."

"That shop is on the way to the water. I will race you there."

We **peel out.** We get to the Stone Hut at the same time. The shop is shut, but we can see a man in there. He lets us come in. The man hands me the ring in a slim plastic bag. I slide the bag with the ring down into my back pants pocket. Then Bob and I speed down to the water. He cuts to the end of the bike path first. That is one for him.

A way off, past some sand dunes, we can see Red Rocks. They are big slabs of red rock that jut up and out over the water. Off the wide end of the rocks, the water is deep and green.

Bob and I lock up our bikes and run down the sand. We get to Red Rocks fast, but I get there first. That is one for me.

Who do you think will win the dive game? Circle your answer.
Bob   Tim   Bob and Tim   Not Bob or Tim
Then read on to find out who can dive deep and win the game.

Out on the end of the rocks, we look down. We can see a long way down into the water. Then we jump in, feet first. The water is as nice as I remember it. It is about as nice as it gets. We swim back over to the sand. Two more times we jump off the rocks, feet first. Then we dive.

I say, "OK, kid, it is time for this dive game. It is time to dive deep . . . all the way down!" Bob gets set to make his dive. It will be a first if Bob or I can make it all the way down.

Bob dives in. He goes down . . . down . . . down. I see him kick to go deep. For a long time there is no sound. Then he comes up fast.

I ask, "Did you make it?"

"I only wish I did. Not this time!" Bob yells up to me. "Come on—go for it!"

I make my dive. Down, down, into the water. I kick my legs to go deep, but no luck. I have to come up. I did not make it all the way down.

We dive a number of times. We get deep but not all the way down. Then we sit on the rocks in the sun. It feels nice to rest. The only sound is the slap of the water on the rocks. We want to keep up the dive game, but it is time to go. So we set out to get our bikes.

I remember the ring and slip my hand into my pocket. The plastic **bag** with the new ring is not there! I feel **grim.** "Bob! This is bad news. The ring is lost!" ▶

You Be the Judge

1. Tim lost the ring at Red Rocks. What should he have done that he did not do? What would you tell him to do now? Write what you think on the lines below.

he should of took the ring straight to his mom when he picked it up.

Think About the Story

Use Story Words

Directions: Look at your list of story words on page 11. Write a story word on each line.

2. Tim did not _remember_ to take the ring from his pocket when he swam.

3. The ring was _new_.

4. The _sound_ of the wind is soft.

5. Bob _only_ wishes he could have dived all the way down.

6. The ring was in a _plastic_ bag.

7. Tim slid the ring into his back _pocket_.

When Did It Happen?

8. Write a number from 1 to 5 in front of each event to show when it happened.

_2_ A man hands Tim the ring in a slim plastic bag.

_1_ Tim and Bob get to the Stone Hut.

_5_ Tim finds that the ring is lost.

_4_ The kids jump in the water, feet first.

_3_ The kids get into a dive game.

Write Sentences About the Story

◆ **Directions:** Circle the word that best fits in each sentence. Then write the sentence on the line.

9. Tim (pick/picks) up an ice cube.

    Tim picks up the ice cube.

10. Bob (toss/tosses) an ice cube at Tim.

    Bob tosses an ice cube at tim.

11. The kids could see Red Rocks past some sand (dune/dunes).

    The kids could see Red rocks past some sand dunes.

12. Bob and Tim (lock/locks) up the bikes.

    Bob and tim lock up the Bikes.

Words and Meanings

◆ **Directions:** Think about how the **bold** words are used in the story. Then circle the words that show the meaning of each word or phrase.

13. In this story, **rods** are _____.
    a. poles to fish with
    b. long sticks
    c. bike spokes

14. When the kids **peel out,** they _____.
    a. peel the plastic from a snack
    b. skid their bike wheels
    c. kick their feet to dive deep

15. To feel **grim** is to feel _____.
    a. bad
    b. glad
    c. fine

Look Ahead

◆ 16. Do you think Tim will get the ring back? How will he do it? Write what you think on the lines below. Then read on to find out what happens.

    yes I think tim will get it back. He will dive in the water to get it.

Letters and Sounds

> **TIP:** When the same two consonants come together at the end of a word, they stand for one sound. **Examples: Mess** ends with the **s** sound. **Will** ends with the **l** sound.

◆ **Directions:** Circle the consonants at the end of each word. Write the sound at the end of each word.

Example: mess   me(ss)   s

1. mi(ss) _Miss_   3. mi(tt) _mitt_   5. stu(ff) _Stuff_

2. wi(ll) _will_   4. fu(zz) _fuzz_

◆ **Directions:** Write the letters on the lines. See how many words you can make.

| gr | k | m | f | b | h | dr | l |

6. _M_ iss   12. _m_ ess   18. _f_ uzz

7. _k_ iss   13. _dr_ ess   19. _b_ uzz

8. _f_ iss   14. _l_ ess

9. _b_ uff   15. _m_ ill

10. _gr_ uff   16. _h_ ill

11. _fl_ uff   17. _k_ ill

Word Bank

Write each of these story words in the Word Bank at the back of this book.

Story Words

◆ **Directions:** Read each word to yourself. Then say the word out loud. Write the word on the line. Check the box after each step.

20. little (lit | tle)   Read ☑ Say ☑ Write ☐   *little*

21. work   Read ☐ Say ☐ Write ☐   *work*

22. know   Read ☐ Say ☐ Write ☐   *know*

23. push   Read ☐ Say ☐ Write ☐   *push*

More Word Work

You can add **ed** to many verbs. Do this to make a verb tell about the past.

Now: Bob and Tim **lock** the bikes.   **The Past:** Bob and Tim **locked** the bikes last week.

◆ **Directions:** Write the sentences below again. Make each one tell about the past. To do this, add **ed** to the **bold** word.

Example: Bees **buzz** by my lunch.

Bees buzzed by my lunch.

24. Nan and Pat **stuff** their socks in a bag.

Nan and Pat stuff their socks in a Bag.

Nan and Pat stuffed their socks in a Bag.

25. The twins **miss** their mom.

The twins miss their mom.

The twins missed their mom.

26. Kids **dress** up for the prom.

Kids dress up for the prom.

Kids dressed up for the prom

DIVE DEEP

"**This is lame stuff,** Bob!" I am not glad about this. The little plastic bag is not in my pocket. It must have worked its way out. How could that be? Why did I not miss it?

"Did you check your pocket twice?" asks Bob.

I check my pocket. All I find is a little tube of sun block and some pocket fuzz. I remember that I stuffed the ring in deep, but it still got out. Now I do not know what to do.

"That sounds bad, Tim." Bob scans the sand dunes. "Do you think the little plastic bag slid out of your pocket and in to the sand?"

I say, "If it did, it will be a big job to find that ring now."

"It may be in the water. I bet it is in the water, Tim!" Bob yells. "I know we need to check in the water!"

We race back up the sand. We cut up to the top of the rocks. Then we look over, down into the water. The deep green water is still. We can see all the way down. Then Bob sees a flash in the water. He yells, "I see it! It flashed in the water. I see it! The ring is down there!"

"Yes, but how will we get it?" I ask. I still feel grim. I feel like this will not work. "What a mess we are in. The ring is all the way down!"

Will Bob and Tim get the ring? Circle your answer.

YES   NO

Then go on to find out.

Bob stands up. "Tim, I know we can get that ring. You and me, now!"

We go and stand on the end of the rock. Bob and I dive deep. We hit the water at the same time. I kick big, as fast as I can. I kick twice. Then I see it. The plastic bag with the ring is way down on the sand. Come on, Tim . . . kick . . . kick . . .

Bob has his hand out. I push my hand out. The little bag with the ring is so close! If I can only **get my mitt on it** . . . but I do not get it. I am still only part way down. It is all over. I have to go up, now!

Then I feel Bob's hand on my back. He pushes me down with one last kick. My hand is still down. I do not know if it will work. My hand goes down a little.

That makes it! I grab the plastic bag and pop back up to the top of the water.

At the top, Bob sees I have the ring. He grins and nods at me. "You win! You made it all the way down!"

"Shut up, you blob!" I say. "You pushed me down! I did it only when you pushed me all the way down! It looks like it takes two to dive deep!"

◆

You Be the Judge

◆ **1.** Do you think Tim needs to tell his mom that the ring fell in the water? Why or why not? Write what you think on the lines below.

No he doesn't cause you found the ring.

Think About the Story

Use Story Words

◆ **Directions:** Look at your list of story words on page 17. Write a story word on each line.

2. Tim did not _Know_ where the ring was.

3. The ring was in a _little_ plastic bag.

4. It takes a lot of _work_ to dive deep!

5. With a _push_ from Bob, Tim went all the way down.

Words and Meanings

◆ **Directions:** Think about how the **bold** words are used in the story. Then circle the words that show the meaning of each word or phrase.

6. Tim said, **"This is lame stuff!"** He means _____.
   a. "This is over!"
   b. "I have a bum leg!"
   c. "This is bad!"

7. In this story, **get my mitt on it** means _____.
   a. grab it with my hand
   b. set my mitt on top of it
   c. toss a mitt to it

8. Tim tells Bob, **"Shut up, you blob!"** Why?
   a. Tim is mad at Bob.
   b. Bob is a blob, and Tim tells him so.
   c. Tim knows Bob helped him a lot.

The Big Idea

9. Which sentence tells what the whole story is about? Write it on the lines.

    a. Two kids go for a swim at Red Rocks.

    b. Two kids must dive deep to get a lost ring.

    c. A man gives Tim a ring in a plastic bag.

Two Kids must dive Deep to get a lost ring.

Why Did It Happen?

Directions: Draw a line from each story event to the reason it happened.

What Happened	Why
10. Bob puts his hand on Tim's back and pushes him down.	He wants to find that ring.
11. Tim checks his pocket.	He knows that the water is too deep for him to dive down and get it.
12. Tim feels grim after he spots the ring.	He wants Tim to go all the way down for the ring.

Write Sentences About the Story

Directions: Use words from the story to answer these questions.

13. Why do the kids go to Red Rocks in the first place?

because They want to.

14. What do the kids like about Red Rocks?

because there rocks that are red.

15. Bob helps Tim get the ring. How?

he helps him swim down to the Bottom

Letters and Sounds

◆ **Directions:** These words have a short vowel sound. Circle the vowel in each word.

1. m(a)d   2. gr(i)m

These words have a long vowel sound. Circle the two vowels in each word.

3. mad(e)   4. gr(i)m(e)

5. What vowel do you see at the end of **made** and **grime**? _e_

> **TIP:** If there are two vowels in a word and one is a final **e**, the first vowel usually stands for a long sound. The final **e** is silent. Words like **made** and **grime** have the consonant-vowel-consonant-**e** pattern. Another way to say consonant-vowel-consonant-**e** is CVC**e**.

◆ **Directions:** Write each word in the box where it belongs.

place	glide	name	prime
glad	skate	time	game
spin	with	back	pack

short *a*	long *a*	short *i*	long *i*
6. place	9. glad	13. with	15. time
7. name	10. pack	14. _____	16. glide
8. skate	11. back		17. prime
	12. game		

◆ **Directions:** Write the letters on the lines. How many words can you make?

f	t	gr	sp	m	l	pr	tr

18. _m_ ade   22. _t_ ime

19. _pr_ ade   23. _l_ ime

20. _gr_ ade   24. _pr_ ime

21. _f_ ade   25. _t_ ime

Story Words

◆ **Directions:** Read each word to yourself. Then say the word out loud. Write the word on the line. Check the box after each step.

26. year   Read ❑ Say ❑ Write ❑   *year*

27. live   Read ❑ Say ❑ Write ❑   *live*

28. helmet (hel|met)   Read ❑ Say ❑ Write ❑   *helmet*

29. turn   Read ❑ Say ❑ Write ❑   *turn*

30. school   Read ❑ Say ❑ Write ❑   *school*

More Word Work

◆ **Directions:** Adding **e** to a word like **mad** changes the vowel sound from short to long. Add an **e** to each word. Then write the vowel sound each new word has.

Examples: mad   made   long a
          grim   grime   long i

31. slid   *slid*   *slide*

32. rid   *rid*   *ride*

33. rat   *rat*   *rate*

34. can   *can*   *cane*

35. bit   *bit*   *bite*

36. glad   *glad*   *glade*

◆ **Directions:** You know that you can add **s** or **es** to many words. Add **s** or **es** to each word below.

37. fish   *fishes*   40. mix   *mixes*

38. fix   *fixs*   41. stand   *stands*

39. bin   *bines*   42. run   *runs*

▶ **Remember!** If a word ends with **x, ch, sh,** or **s,** add **es** instead of **s.**

Use What You Know

Jessie and Jade like to skate, but many shops and schools will not let kids skate there. What do you think is a good place for kids to skate? Write what you think on the lines below.

Kids Should Skate at a skating ring.

A PLACE TO SKATE

"Jessie, are you all set? Get that skate on. Can we go now?" Jade sped past Jessie on her skates. Her red helmet seemed to whiz by in a mad flash. She came up fast and made a turn. "It is time to skate!" she yelled.

Jessie gave a tug to her left skate. "Are you going to get mad about it, Jade? **Rats!** Come on, skate!" She pushed in to the skate. At last it went on all the way. "I tell you, **these new blades fit me first rate.**" This year was her first year on skates. Jessie flicked a bit of grime from her green and black helmet. She got the helmet on. She jumped up and pushed fast to skate up to Jade. Jessie checked her pads as she came to a stop.

"OK, Jessie," said Jade. "Two blocks down the hill is a flat place with a step. It is by some shops. I bet we can skate there."

"We *would* live on a hill! This place is not the best for skates," said Jessie. She pushed off. "If I use the brakes, I can make it down the hill."

Jade and Jessie made it to the shops. Jessie was no flash on the way down. She fell twice and bumped her helmet one time. But she did not get mad. She just got up and went on. Jade had a fast ride down and made a spin at the end. At the shops, she slid in fast and jumped. She landed up on the step and made a slide. At the end of the step was a ramp. She came down the ramp and made a spin to stop.

"Nice glide, Jade! With time, I may skate like you!" Jessie slid in to the flat part. She got up by the step to fake a jump.

A man came out of one of the shops. "You kids! You have to get out, now! You may not skate in this place! It is a crime to skate by these shops."

"A crime?" said Jade. She gave a look to Jessie. Jade looked mad. "But kids like to skate!" she said. "We have got to have a place to skate! And we live in a place that is all hills!"

"Yes, I know," said the man. "Still, you have to go—and go now."

"Jade, we can find a place to skate," said Jessie. "I know we can."

Will Jade and Jessie find a place to skate? Circle your answer.

YES **NO**

Then keep going to find out what takes place.

Jade gave a grim look to Jessie. "We can look at the shops down the street," said Jade.

The two pushed off into the street. They made their way over to some new shops. It was the same thing as at the first shops. They got kicked out.

Jade looked sad. She sat down at the side of the hill. Jessie sat by her.

"What about the school?" Jessie said. "We can go skate there."

Jade looked up. The school was a **prime** place to skate. It had lots of ramps, steps, crates, and other fine things to skate on. "It could work," she said. She jumped up and gave Jessie a smile. "Race you?"

"Not yet, Jade! This is my first year on skates, remember?" Jessie was glad to see Jade smile.

At the school, no one was out and about. The place was all theirs. For a time the only sound was one of skates and turns and slides. Jessie **worked up to** a little jump. She jumped and slid on a step.

"You, there . . . you kids!" A man came out of the shade. "My name is Nate James. I work at this school. It is not OK to skate at this place."

"Mr. James, is there no place we can skate?" said Jade. "All the shops say it is not OK. Now you say it is not OK at the school. We like to skate. The place we live is all hills. What can we do?"

Nate James looked at Jade and Jessie. He said, "It is a shame that kids have no place to skate. I have to kick a lot of kids on skates out of this place. I do not like to do it, but it is my job."

For a time, no one said a thing. "I tell you what," said Mr. James at last. "I may know of a way to get you kids a place to skate." ▶

You Be the Judge

◆ 1. Do you think it is a crime to skate by shops? Why or why not? Write what you think on the lines below.

no I don't think so cause you can skate anywhere you want.

2. What can the kids do to find a place to skate?

they can look around for a place to skate or raise money.

Think About the Story

Use Story Words

◆ **Directions:** Look at your list of story words on page 23. Write a story word on each line.

3. There are lots of hills where Jade and Jessie *live* .

4. It was Jessie's first *year* on skates.

5. The kids went to the *school* to skate.

6. Kids who skate need to have a *helmet* .

7. Jade made a fast *turn* on her blades.

Write Sentences About the Story

◆ **Directions:** Circle the word that best fits in each sentence. Then write the sentence on the line.

8. The man said, "It (is/be) a crime to skate by these shops!"

The man said It is a crime to skate by these shops.

9. Jade and Jessie (is/are) pals.

Jade and Jessie are pals.

10. Jessie (work/worked) up to a little jump.

Jessie worked up a little Jump.

11. Nate James (kick/kicks) the kids out.

Nate James kicks the kids out.

The Big Idea

◆ **12.** Which sentence tells what the whole story is about? Write it on the lines.

    a. Jade and Jessie get new skates at the same time.

    b. Jade and Jessie live in a place that is all hills.

    c. Jade and Jessie want a place where it is OK to skate.

Jade and Jessie want a place where it is ok to skate.

Words and Meanings

◆ **Directions:** Think about how the **bold** words are used in the story. Then circle the words that show the meaning of each word or phrase.

13. Jessie says, **"These new blades fit me first rate."** What does she mean?

    a. The skates are the first ones she has had.

    b. The skates fit very well.

    c. Her blades are the best ones you can find.

14. Jessie says, **"Rats!"** She means _____.

    a. "Oh no!"

    b. "Look out! I see rats!"

    c. "Good!"

15. A **prime** place to skate is a _____.

    a. first place to skate

    b. bad place to skate

    c. fine place to skate

16. Jessie **worked up to** a little jump. This means that she _____.

    a. made a lot of fast little jumps

    b. took her skates to work with her

    c. did a little bit at a time, and then a little more

Look Ahead

◆ **17.** What will Mr. James tell the kids next? Write what you think on the lines below. Read on to find out if you are right.

he will help them find a place to skate.

Letters and Sounds

◆ **Directions:** These words have the long **e** sound. Circle the vowel or vowels in each word.

1. s(ee)d   2. sh(e)   3. b(ea)d

> ▶ **TIP:** The letters **ee, e,** and **ea** can all stand for the long **e** sound.

◆ **Directions:** Read these words. Circle each one that has the long **e** sound.

4. n(ee)d	7. slide	10. b(ee)	13. send
5. net	8. n(ea)t	11. line	14. s(e)t
6. rent	9. b(e)	12. bake	15. b(ea)n

◆ **Directions:** Write each word you circled under the word below that has the same pattern of letters for long **e.**

mean	she	seen
16. need	18. bee	19. be
17. neat		20. bean

◆ **Directions:** Write the letters on the lines. See how many words you can make.

f	s	b	sh	h	n	m	tr

21. __b__ e   24. __n__ eat   27. __n__ eed

22. __m__ e   25. __m__ eat   28. __s__ eed

23. __sh__ e   26. __tr__ eat   29. __f__ eed

Story Words

◆ **Directions:** Read each word to yourself. Then say the word out loud. Write the word on the line. Check the box after each step.

30. give   Read ☐ Say ☐ Write ☐   *give*

31. most   Read ☐ Say ☐ Write ☐   *most*

32. very (ver | y)   Read ☐ Say ☐ Write ☐   *very*

33. city (ci | ty)   Read ☐ Say ☐ Write ☐   *city*

34. woman (wo | man)   Read ☐ Say ☐ Write ☐   *woman*

Word Bank

Write each of these story words in the Word Bank at the back of this book.

More Word Work

You can add **ing** to many verbs. Do this to make a verb tell about something that is going on now.

The Past: Tom **locked** his bike.   **Now:** Tom **is locking** his bike.

◆ 35. What word was added to the sentence that tells about now? *is*

◆ **Directions:** Add **ing** to each word. Then write the word in the sentence.

Example: look   **looking** → Tim is **looking** at me.

36. dress   *dress*   → Little kids like *dressing* up.

37. wish   *wish*   → Sam is *wishing* for a new bike.

38. send   *send*   → Nan is *sending* me a note.

◆ **Directions:** You know that adding **ed** to a verb makes it tell about the past. Write these sentences again. Make each verb tell about the past.

39. I miss my pals a lot.

I missed my pals a lot.

40. Dan and Jade lock their bikes up.

Dan and Jade Locked their bikes up.

41. I call my dog Nate.

I called my dog Nate.

42. Dave and Viv rent bikes from that man.

Dave and Viv rented bikes From that man

THE SKATE RAMP

Nate James turned to look out over the school land. Past the school was a lot that had a little hill and some green shade trees on it. He gave a nod at the little hill. "Do you kids see that lot over there? I know the woman who has that lot. Her name is Mim Steed. It may be that she would let kids use the land. If she did, and if the city gives its OK, we could set up a skate place over there. What if we go take a look now at that lot?"

Jade and Jessie could not keep the grins off their faces. At the same time, they said, "Can we?"

Jessie and Jade pushed off very fast on their skates, speeding to lead Mr. James to the lot. Over at the lot, the only sound was of water in a little creek at the side of the lot. "This is **neat,** Mr. James!" said Jade. "I could see this as a very neat skate place! See, most of the lot is very flat. The other part, the hill, is like a big ramp."

Not to be beat, Jessie jumped in. "On that hill, you could get up some speed on skates. And those little bumps over there would make very fine jumps!"

"We could make other things on the flat part, like a fun box. It's a box to jump up and slide on," said Jade. "We could make ramps, and steps, and **pipes** with steep sides!"

Mr. James cut in. "You know, if kids speed very fast, it may not be safe! The people who live and work in this city will feel that kids need a safe place to do things."

"But all the kids would need to keep on their helmets and pads and things," said Jessie. "We do! We use helmets and pads all the time!"

Will Jade and Jessie do the work needed to get a new place to skate? Circle your answer.

YES   **NO**

Then read on to find out.

"I will go see Mrs. Steed for you. But I will give you a big hint," said Mr. James. "You will need to get as many kids as you can to write to Mrs. Steed and the city. You will need to get most of the people of the city to give their OK for a skate place for kids. It may take most of the year to get people to give their OK. What I mean is, you may need to work a very long time for this."

"We can do all that work, Mr. James," said Jessie. "Most kids we know like to skate. We know at least 50 kids! And we can find other kids and get them to write."

"OK," said Mr. James. "I will see what I can do."

In a week, Nate James got to see Mrs. Steed about the lot. Mrs. Steed said it was a fine plan. She would give her OK if the city would give its OK. The city meeting was set two weeks from that day. Jessie and Jade had many kids write to the city. At last it was the day of the city meeting.

Mr. James, Jessie, Jade, and Mrs. Steed all came to the meeting. Jessie and Jade had on their skates, helmets, and pads. They did this so people could see how they would skate and be safe. They each got up to speak about the new place to skate. They said what a neat deed it would be to make a safe place for kids to skate. They said that kids would need to use their helmets and pads to keep safe.

The city people looked on from their seats. In the end, they did not say no to the skate place. On the other hand, they did not yet say yes. They said, "We will take a look at that lot. We will have to find out what other people would like. We will look over your plans to see if they will work. In a little time, who knows, we may have a place for kids to skate in this city."

Jessie and Jade looked at Mr. James and Mrs. Steed. They all looked glad.

"I know that I would like a place NOW to skate," said Jade. "And I know it may be a long time from now that the OK comes from the city. But for now, Mrs. Steed, at least we can thank you. Thank you for being willing to give us your lot as a place to skate!"

You Be the Judge

1. The city did not just give its OK when the kids asked. Do you think it is best for the city to take a look at the lot and think about it for a time? Why or why not? Write what you think on the lines below.

No cause the kids want a lot now.

Think About the Story

Use Story Words

Directions: Look at your list of story words on page 29. Write a story word on each line.

2. A _woman_ named Mrs. Steed has a lot.

3. Mr. James thinks Mrs. Steed may _give_ her OK for the plan.

4. The _city_ needs to say OK to the skate place, too.

5. _most_ of the lot is flat.

6. Jessie and Jade are _very_ safe when they skate.

When Did It Happen?

7. Write a number from 1 to 4 in front of each event to show when it happened.

_4_ The kids go to a city meeting.

_2_ Jessie and Jade skate to the school.

_1_ A man tells Jade and Jessie they may not skate by the shops.

_3_ Mr. James meets with Mrs. Steed.

What Were the Facts?

8. Why did Jade and Jessie like Mrs. Steed's lot? Circle the reasons.

   a. Most of it was hills.
   (b.) Most of it was flat.
   (c.) It had a little creek on it.
   d. It had one hill that could make a ramp.
   (e.) It had little bumps that could make fine jumps.

Write Sentences About the Story

◆ **Directions:** Circle the word that best fits in each sentence. Then write the sentence on the line.

9. Jade and Jessie could not (**keep**/keeps) the grins off their faces.

Jade and Jessie could not keep the grins of there faces

10. Jessie was (speed/**speeding**) to the lot.

Jessie was speeding to the lot

11. The people who (live/**lives**) in the city want kids to be safe.

The people who lives in the city want kids to be safe

Words and Meanings

◆ **Directions:** Think about how the **bold** words are used in the story. Then circle the words that show the meaning of each word or phrase.

12. Jade wants ramps, steps, and **pipes** with steep sides. Here, **pipes** are _____.
   a. thin things that hold water
   b. places for skate tricks
   c. chimes that make soft sounds

13. Jade said, "This is **neat**, Mr. James!" Here, **neat** means _____.
   a. very fine
   b. not picked up
   c. a mess

Why Did It Happen?

◆ **Directions:** Draw a line from each story event to the reason it happened.

What Happened	Why
14. Jessie and Jade got lots of kids to write to the city.	○ They wanted the people to know that kids will skate safe.
15. Jessie and Jade had their helmets on at the city meeting.	○ They may get a place to skate after all.
16. Jessie and Jade were glad at the end of the meeting.	○ They wanted the city to OK plans for a skate place.

Letters and Sounds

◆ **Directions:** These words have a short vowel sound. Circle the vowel in each word.

1. h(o)p   2. d(u)d

These words have a long vowel sound. Circle the two vowels in each word.

3. h(o)p(e)   4. d(u)de

5. What vowel do you see at the end of **hope** and **dude**? _e_

Remember: If there are two vowels in a word and one is a final **e**, the first vowel usually stands for a long sound. The final **e** is silent.

◆ **Directions:** Write each word in the box where it belongs.

stop   cute   flute   sock
cut   strut   stones   use
sole   mute   broke   chute

short o	long o	short u	long u
6. broke	8. stop	11. mute	13. strut
7. sole	9. sock	12. cute	14. cut
	10. stones		15. flute
			16. use
			17. chute

◆ **Directions:** Write the letters on the lines. How many words can you make?

| fl | p | r | cl | n | m | c | br |

18. _n_ ose   22. _fl_ ute

19. _r_ ose   23. _c_ ute

20. _p_ ose   24. _m_ ute

21. _fl_ ose   25. _br_ ute

Story Words

Directions: Read each word to yourself. Then say the word out loud. Write the word on the line. Check the box after each step.

26. after (af | ter)   Read ☑ Say ☑ Write ☑   *after*

27. our   Read ☑ Say ☑ Write ☑   *our*

28. grind   Read ☑ Say ☑ Write ☑   *grind*

29. open (o | pen)   Read ☑ Say ☑ Write ☑   *open*

More Word Work

You know that you can add **ed** and **ing** to many verbs. Here's how to add **ed** or **ing** to a verb that ends in **e**.

$$skate + ed = skated$$
$$skate + ing = skating$$

30. What letter was dropped from the word **skate** when the endings were added? _____ *e*

> **TIP:** When adding **ed** or **ing** to a word that ends in **e**, drop the **e**. Then add the ending.

Directions: Add **ed** and **ing** to each word below.

Example: close   *closed*   *closing*

	ed	ing
31. use	*Closed*	*closeing*
32. pose	*Posed*	*Poseing*
33. mute	*muted*	*muteing*
34. doze	*dozed*	*dozeing*
35. rate	*rated*	*rateing*
36. like	*liked*	*likeing*

Use What You Know

Next you will read an ad for a job at a skate shop. What do you find in a job ad? Write what you think on the lines below.

where it is

How much they pay

What hours you work

what days you work

SKATE SHOP JOB

What can you tell about this job from this shot? Does it look like a fun job or a dull one? Write what you think, and why, on the lines below.

it looks like a fun Job. cause you get to rollerblade.

Read on to find out more about the job.

Ramp Up Skating and Chute City Skate Shop
Has a Job for You!

Skating Dudes! Skating Gals!

Some people just live to skate. Are you one of them?
Are you **tuned in to skating?** Would you like to work with
and know a little more about skating?

After School Jobs to Open Up at Ramp Up Skating and Chute City Skate Shop!

We are a **top grade** skate place and skate shop. Now you can
use what you know about skating. Turn your fun into fun work!
First of all, we need people who like skates and skating. We have
some after school jobs coming up in May and June.
Most of our jobs will go all year.

What the Jobs Are:

- Sell skates, wheels, trucks, **sole plates,** grind plates.
- Sell other skating stuff, like helmets and pads.
- Set up and fix skates.
- Teach skating classes.
- Teach people how to skate in a safe way.
- Pose doing skate tricks. (Can you do a mute grab? How about grabs, spins, grinds, and jumps?)
- Clean up the skating place and shop.
- Keep the skating stuff neat.
- Open or close the shop if needed.

More About Our Skate Jobs

- Other skills for these jobs:
  - Be on time!
  - Look neat!
  - Like to work with all kinds of people!
  - Keep your grades up at school! (Must make at least a C in most classes.)
- When the jobs are:
  - Most of our jobs are part time, after school.
  - On the week end, you may be working all day.
- Our shop opens at 9 A.M.
  - We close at 7 P.M. each day.
- Where we are and who to see:
  130 West Flute Way
  Chute City
  377-455-6633
  Who to see about these jobs: Liz Rose

What Do You Think?

◆ 1. Do you think a job at a skate shop would be fun? Why or why not? Write what you think on the lines below.

Yes I think it will be
Fun cause I like rollarblading.

Think About the Ad

Use Words from the Ad

◆ **Directions:** Look at your list of story words on page 35. Write a story word on each line.

2. Some jobs are for ___after___ school.

3. The word ___Open___ means "not closed."

4. A ___grind___ is a skating trick.

5. The stuff that is mine and yours is ___our___ stuff.

What Are the Facts?

◆ **Directions:** Which sentences tell about the skate shop jobs? Which sentences do not? Cross out the sentences that do not tell about the jobs.

6. ~~The jobs end in May or June.~~

7. It is fun work.

8. ~~Kids do no selling, just teaching.~~

9. People need to like and know skating.

10. All the jobs go all year long.

What Can You Tell?

◆ 11. What are the bosses at the Chute City Skate Shop looking for? Circle your answers.

   a. They want kids who do OK in school.

   b. They want kids who look neat.

   c. They want kids who are new to skating.

   (d.) They want kids who know all there is to know about skating.

Write About the Ad

◆ **Directions:** Use words from the ad to answer these questions.

12. When does the skate shop open and close?

   9 A.M. - 7 P.m.

13. What is one skill people must have to get a job at the skate shop?

   Be on time.

   _____

14. What are two things people must teach in this job?

   Set up and fix skates,

   open and close shop if needed.

15. What are some things people must sell in this job?

   Skates, hemets and wheels.

   _____

16. Who would you ask for if you wanted to chat about the job?

   Liz Rose

Words and Meanings

◆ **Directions:** Think about how the **bold** words are used in the ad. Then circle the words that show the meaning of each word or phrase.

17. The ad says the skate shop is **top grade**. This means that the shop _____.
   a. is the best a skate shop can be
   b. only has kids with good grades
   c. has a steep skating ramp

18. In the ad, a **sole plate** is _____.
   a. a plate of fish
   b. a skating trick
   c. part of a skate

19. If you are **tuned in to skating,** _____.
   a. you like tunes about skating
   b. you know a little about skating
   c. you are a big skating fan

Letters and Sounds

Skate has one syllable. **Skating** has two syllables.

skate	skat	ing
1	1	2

Man has one syllable. **Magnet** has two syllables.

man	mag	net
1	1	2

Directions: Read each word. Write 1 or 2 on the line to tell how many syllables are in it.

Examples: went 1   people 2

1. work _1_   6. sound _1_
2. only _2_   7. little _2_
3. over _2_   8. number _2_
4. part _1_   9. calling _2_
5. brick _1_   10. back _1_

11. How many consonant sounds do you hear in the middle of **skating**? _2_

12. How many consonant sounds do you hear in the middle of **magnet**? _2_

Directions: Circle the consonant or consonants you see in the middle of these words. Then write how many consonant sounds you hear in the middle of each word.

Examples: ba(sk)et 2   wa(t)er 1   ca(ll)er 1

13. sk(at)ing _2_   16. pla(st)ic _2_   19. su(dd)en _1_

14. ma(gn)et _2_   17. he(lm)et _2_   20. o(p)en _1_

15. ci(t)y _1_   18. a(ft)er _1_   21. ve(r)y _1_

Story Words

Directions: Read each word to yourself. Then say the word out loud. Write the word on the line. Check the box after each step.

Word Bank

Write each of these story words in the Word Bank at the back of this book.

22. good   Read ❑ Say ❑ Write ❑ _good_
23. think   Read ❑ Say ❑ Write ❑ _think_
24. car   Read ❑ Say ❑ Write ❑ _car_
25. interview   Read ❑ Say ❑ Write ❑ _interview_
    (in | ter | view)
26. application   Read ❑ Say ❑ Write ❑ _application_
    (ap | pli | ca | tion)

More Word Work

You know that you can add **ed** and **ing** to many words. What happens when you add **ed** or **ing** to a word like **grab**? Here's what happens:

    grab + ed = grabbed   grab + ing = grabbing

27. What letter was added to **grab** when the endings were added? _ed_

> **TIP:** When adding **ed** or **ing** to a word with a short vowel sound that ends in one consonant, double the last consonant.

Directions: Add **ed** and **ing** to each word below.

Example: bug   bugged   bugging

	ed	ing
28. bat	bated	bating
29. pin	pined	pining
30. skid	skided	skiding
31. jab	Jabed	Jabing
32. stop	stoped	stoping
33. sub	subed	subing
34. grab	grabed	grabing

Use What You Know

The kid who tells this story wants to get a job at a race track. How do you think a kid could help out at a race track?

_____

_____

_____

_____

RACE TRACK DREAMS

Travis and I are standing on the top seats looking down at the **track.** Sixteen race cars speed down the track. Making a whining sound, they whiz past. I am seeing the cars, but inside, I am dreaming.

. . . Big Don Cole speeds down the last lap. Smoke is streaming out the back of his green race car, number 2. . . . The people in the stands see only the flash of sun on his plastic helmet as he whizzes past. Coming into the turn, Cole is skidding past the black car, number 19. . . . Now he is **grabbing the lead** from the red car, number 4. . . . Will he make it? He is coming down the speed way. . . . It is very close. Yes! There he goes! . . . Big Don Cole wins the race!

All of a sudden, I feel my sides being jabbed. "Wake up, dude!" says Travis. "I think we just missed your meeting about the job!" Travis looks mad, then smiles. "Just kidding! But you and I need to get going. It is time for your interview with Dale Haskins."

It is a good thing that Travis remembered the time. After all, I have been planning this day for weeks. It would be a shame to mess up by missing my job interview. Travis has a job at the track. Now I am hoping to get a job at the track. I like to be with the race cars. I want most of all to drive the race cars.

"Do you still have your job application?" asks Travis. "Is it all filled out?" He gives me a good long look.

"Yep, I filled it out at school," I say. The application is hidden in my pocket. Part of me is still dreaming about driving a race car. Some day, I think, I will drive a race car!

We make our way down to the interview place. We are very close to the track now. I like the sounds of the race cars mixed with the smells of gas, smoke, and oil.

Other kids are lined up in the shade by the stands. We push open the gate and go over to get in line. After a while, we are first in line. A man comes out and waves Travis and me in.

Do you think Don will get a job at the race track? Circle your answer. YES NO

Then keep reading to find out what happens.

"Don, this is Dale Haskins," says Travis. "Mr. Haskins, this is Don Cole." Travis turns me over to Haskins. I hand Haskins my application. He looks it over. At last, he looks at me.

"OK, I see you live close to City Speed Way, like Travis," says Haskins. "Good. Do you drive?"

"Yes! I have been driving for a year." I am thinking, Just let me get in to the seat of one of those race cars! I will let you see how I can drive!

"Well, we need some kids to drive," says Haskins.

Travis asks, "Race cars, Mr. Haskins?"

"**Very cute, Travis,** but no, not the race cars. Those are not part of this job."

I feel a little sad about this, but Mr. Haskins keeps going. "In this job you would just be on hand all day to drive people places. You could be driving to places at the race track. Or you could go some place out and about in the city. What about two days from now? Can you come in then?"

I say, "You bet, Mr. Haskins!"

"OK, good. For now, I will have Travis drive you all over the track. He will take you to all the places you could need to drive to on the job. Then you will know how to find your way about."

I am thinking, Is this good or what! I will be so close to the race cars. And what if I can just sneak a little time to sit in one of them!

Mr. Haskins is ending our interview. He is giving me some tips. "And just remember, you do not get to drive the race cars!" ▶

You Be the Judge

◀▶ **1.** Do you think Don is a good kid for this job? Why or why not? Write what you think on the lines below.

_____

_____

Think About the Story

Use Story Words

◀▶ **Directions:** Look at your list of story words on page 41. Write a story word on each line.

2. Don had his job _____ hidden in his pocket.

3. An _____ is a time to speak to a boss about getting a job.

4. Don wants to drive a race _____.

5. Mr. Haskins tells Don that it is _____ that he lives close to the track.

6. Travis and Don _____ the race track is a fun place to spend time.

The Big Idea

◀▶ **7.** Which sentence tells what the whole story is about? Write it on the lines.

a. Travis and Don go to the race track.

b. Don dreams about driving race cars.

c. Don wants to get a job at the race track.

_____

_____

When Did It Happen?

◀▶ **8.** Write a number from 1 to 4 in front of each event to show when it happened.

_____ Travis takes Don all over the track.

_____ Don and Travis go to the track.

_____ Don fills out his job application.

_____ Don meets Dale Haskins.

Write Sentences About the Story

◆ **Directions:** Use words from the story to answer these questions.

9. What will Don do at his job?

_____

_____

10. Don wishes he could do one thing that is not part of the job. What is it?

_____

11. What is one way Travis helps Don?

_____

_____

Words and Meanings

◆ **Directions:** Think about how the **bold** words are used in the story. Then circle the words that show the meaning of each word or phrase.

12. Which word means the same as **track**?
    a. line up
    b. race way
    c. street car

13. Mr. Haskins says, **"Very cute, Travis."** He means _____.
    a. "You look cute."
    b. "Good thinking, Travis."
    c. "You must be joking."

14. In the dream Don has, he is **grabbing the lead**. This means he is _____.
    a. taking first place in the race
    b. crossing the finish line first
    c. grabbing the lead car with his hand

Look Ahead

◆ 15. Do you think Don will like the job? Do you think Mr. Haskins will like Don? Write what you think on the lines below. Read on to find out if you are right.

_____

_____

Letters and Sounds

◆ **Directions:** Circle the two consonants at the beginning of each word.

1. drop   **2.** slope   **3.** skim   **4.** snap   **5.** click

In these words, each consonant stands for its own sound.

◆ **Directions:** Two consonants can come together at the end of a word. Circle the two consonants at the end of each word.

6. help   **7.** gulp   **8.** gasp   **9.** dust   **10.** lost

In these words, each consonant stands for its own sound. To read these words, blend the sounds together.

◆ **Directions:** Read these words. Write how many consonant sounds you hear at the end of each word.

Examples: fluff   1   risk   2

11. ask _____   **17.** clasp _____

12. mess _____   **18.** fuzz _____

13. milk _____   **19.** mask _____

14. elk _____   **20.** cast _____

15. list _____   **21.** miss _____

16. fizz _____   **22.** last _____

◆ **Directions:** Write the letters on the lines. See how many words you can make.

g	c	l	cl	b	gr	f	m

23. _____ asp   **26.** _____ ast   **29.** _____ elt

24. _____ asp   **27.** _____ ast   **30.** _____ elt

25. _____ asp   **28.** _____ ast   **31.** _____ elt

Word Bank

Write each of these story words in the Word Bank at the back of this book.

Story Words

◆ **Directions:** Read each word to yourself. Then say the word out loud. Write the word on the line. Check the box after each step.

32. sentence (sen | tence)   Read ❑ Say ❑ Write ❑ _____

33. say   Read ❑ Say ❑ Write ❑ _____

34. great   Read ❑ Say ❑ Write ❑ _____

35. where   Read ❑ Say ❑ Write ❑ _____

36. through   Read ❑ Say ❑ Write ❑ _____

More Word Work

◆ **Directions:** You know that a word can have more than one syllable. Look at these two-syllable words. Circle the vowels in each word.

Example: b(a)t t(e)d

37. magnet   38. biggest   39. after   40. running

41. How many vowels did you find in each word? _____

▶ **TIP:** Every syllable has a vowel.

Splitting longer words into syllables can help you read them. Here is how to split these words:

mag | net   big | gest   af | ter   run | ning

◆ **Directions:** Try splitting the words below into syllables. To do this, write each word. Put a line in between the two consonants in the middle of the word.

Example: winning   win | ning

42. swimming _____   45. skidded _____

43. mascot _____   46. bobcat _____

44. witness _____   47. kidding _____

▶ **TIP:** The letters **th** in words like **with** always stay together. So do the letters **sh** in words like **wish**.

wish | es   dish | es   with | out

THE PACE CAR

"Say, what? Where did you say to go?" I have to yell to Haskins over the sound of the cars.

Haskins gets up close to say the sentence one more time. He is asking me to go stock the **press** box with snacks. He says to go in the back way and take out the old stuff and stock up with new snacks.

I have been working at the race track for some time now. It is a great job. Turns out the job is not all about driving. It is about running for this, running for that. Most days it is just go do this and go do that. It is **the same old grind**—OK work, but not a lot of big fun. But on race days— well, things can get good on those days. On race days, Travis and I may get to help out the VIPs. These people are the top names in racing and the big bosses at the track. Or I may get to look at the race from one of the pits. At times, things have to happen very fast. Take the time some kid lost track of the prize cup. At the end of the race, we all had to look all about—and fast—to find it.

I go over to the press box. Only then I see that a TV interview is going on. I do not know what to do. One of the rules is not to go through the press box if TV stuff is going on. I see all the TV people in there. Some of them are dudes I have seen on TV! Well, I think, after all, it is my job. My boss said to go in there now. So I go in. I sneak past as fast as I can. I check the snacks and take out the old things. I get the new stuff in there. Then I get lost fast, but I am grinning. I think, I will have to look for my face on TV.

On my way back to Haskins, I see two great new race cars. No one is looking. I would like to get in to that seat! I can just feel how it is to sit in back of the wheel. If only I could go for a fast little ride in this thing! What about that? No one would know!

What do you think? Will Don drive the race car? Circle your answer.

YES   NO

Then keep reading to find out what happens.

You know, I just about do it. I am so close. I have my hand on the car. I want in the biggest way to get in to that car! Only just then, Haskins buzzes me to come on back in. I gulp. I have the feeling he can see me! I swipe some dust off the car, giving it a pat. Then I run off, thinking, OK, where am I off to now?

When I get back to Haskins, he says, "Don, how would you like to do a new thing? We need to get our race track pace car cleaned. We need it back by two." Then came the best sentence of all: "I need you to drive the pace car over to the city and get it cleaned through and through." He is telling me to drive the pace car!

"You have to be fast," Haskins says. "Can you get through and back by two?"

Say what! I am so jazzed. The pace car is just like a race car. It leads the other cars in the first **lap** of the race. This is great! "You bet, Mr. Haskins!"

I open the car and slide in back of the wheel. This feels good! I am going to be driving the pace car. I have the biggest smile on my face. Look out, people! Big Don Cole is coming through!

You Be the Judge

◆ **1.** Do you think Don is doing great on the job? Or do you think he is doing just OK? Why? Write what you think on the lines below.

_____

_____

Think About the Story

Use Story Words

◆ **Directions:** Look at your list of story words on page 47. Write a story word on each line.

2. This is made up of words. _____

3. This means "very, very fine." _____

4. This means "speak." _____

5. Use this word to tell about a place. _____

6. This means "in one end and out the other." _____

Write Sentences About the Story

◆ **Directions:** Use words from the story to answer these questions.

7. Mr. Haskins and Don have to yell at each other. Why?

_____

_____

8. Why do things get more fun on race days?

_____

_____

9. Don gulps when Mr. Haskins buzzes him. Why?

_____

_____

Why Did It Happen?

◆ **Directions:** Draw a line from each story event to the reason it happened.

What Happened	Why
10. Don thinks his job is just OK.	○ Haskins asks Don to drive the pace car.
11. Don gets jazzed.	○ Don thinks his face may be on TV.
12. Don grins after he stocks snacks in the press box.	○ The job is not about driving at all.

Words and Meanings

◆ **Directions:** Think about how the **bold** words are used in the story. Then circle the words that show the meaning of each word or phrase.

13. In this story, **lap** means _____.
    a. a trip around a race track
    b. a place for little kids to sit
    c. a dog drinking water

14. In this story, **press** means _____.
    a. push down on
    b. a TV interview
    c. people who have TV and news jobs

15. Don tells us that his job is **the same old grind**. He means that the job _____.
    a. is the same all the time, and it gets old
    b. is fun most of the time
    c. grinds him down each day

When Did It Happen?

◆ 16. Write a number from 1 to 5 in front of each event to show when it happened.

_____ Don sees two new race cars.

_____ Mr. Haskins asks Don to do a new job.

_____ Don gets in the pace car and grins.

_____ Don stocks the snacks in the press box.

_____ Mr. Haskins buzzes Don.

Letters and Sounds

◆ **Directions:** You know that **a, e, i, o,** and **u** are vowels. The letter **y** can act as a vowel, too. Read these words. Circle the **y** in each one.

1. only   2. my

◆ **Directions:** Finish these sentences. Use the words above.

3. **Y** has a long **i** sound in the word _____.

4. **Y** has a long **e** sound in the word _____.

◆ **Directions:** Circle the **y** in each word. Then write **long i** or **long e** to tell what vowel sound **y** has.

Examples: h a p p y̶ long e   fl y̶ long i

5. neatly _____   9. flying _____

6. silly _____   10. dry _____

7. cry _____   11. funny _____

8. by _____   12. openly _____

◆ **Directions:** Find three pairs of words that rhyme. Write them on the lines.

crying   funny
penny   many
sunny   drying

13. _____   _____

14. _____   _____

15. _____   _____

Story Words

Word Bank

Write each of these story words in the Word Bank at the back of this book.

◆ **Directions:** Read each word to yourself. Then say the word out loud. Write the word on the line. Check the box after each step.

16. much   Read ❑ Say ❑ Write ❑ _____

17. before (be │ fore)   Read ❑ Say ❑ Write ❑ _____

18. right   Read ❑ Say ❑ Write ❑ _____

19. apply (ap │ ply)   Read ❑ Say ❑ Write ❑ _____

20. along (a │ long)   Read ❑ Say ❑ Write ❑ _____

More Word Work

You can add the ending **ly** to some words. The ending **ly** means "in a way that is."

Neatly means "in a way that is neat."

Openly means "in a way that is open."

◆ **Directions:** Add **ly** to these words. Then use the new word to finish each sentence.

Example: neat   neatly → I stacked my socks neatly.

21. bad _____ → I need a bike _____.

22. grim _____ → Ann looked _____ at
                           the leak and the wet mess.

23. sad _____ → Tim _____ looked for
                          his lost cat.

24. part _____ → The glass is _____ filled
                           with water.

◆ **Directions:** You know that you can add **ed** and **ing** to many words. Add them to these words.

	ed	ing
25. hike	_____	_____
26. wish	_____	_____
27. dim	_____	_____
28. rent	_____	_____

GETTING A JOB

So you would like to try to get a job? Great! But how much do you know about the steps to getting a job? Is there a right way to do things? What are the best ways to go about it? These tips can take you along from application through interview.

Filling Out a Job Application

For most jobs, you will be asked to fill out an application. You must fill out the application and turn it in before you get an interview.

Before You Go to Apply for a Job

Make up a fact sheet at home, before you go to apply. These are facts all about you. Bring your fact sheet to help you fill out job applications. These are the types of facts to write:

▲ **All about me:** List your name, your address, and a number to reach you.

▲ **My schools:** How much school have you had? List the names, places, and dates of your schooling.

▲ **My jobs:** List where and when you worked, and what you did.

▲ **People who know me well:** List the names and numbers of those people.

▲ **Why I would like this job:** Write a sentence or two about why this job would be good for you, and why you would be right for the job. List the skills you have that can help you do this job right.

When You Go to Apply for a Job

▲ Look over the application and see what it says, line by line. Fill out each line fully.

▲ Write neatly. People who do not know you will be reading the application.

▲ You may be asked to say why you would like the job. Write in sentences, if you have space.

Going for a Job Interview

Remember these tips when meeting people you may be working for, or with:

▲ **Dress neatly.** The people you meet will be seeing you for the very first time. They may go on what they see. In other words, most work places like to have people looking neat and clean. Remember, very hip and flashy dress is not the right look for most job interviews.

▲ **Bring just yourself, and yourself only.** Things like gum, CDs, and other people are best left at home or in the car.

▲ **Smile, and mean it.** Be open with your good will. Being happy, liking life, and getting along well with others are real job skills.

▲ **When speaking, look right at the people you are meeting with.** The people interviewing you are trying to get to know you. They are trying to see how well you will fit in with the job and the work place. After all, they are thinking about how well you will do at this job. They are thinking about how you will get along with others. They will ask things. Answer them openly.

▲ **Say what you would like to get out of working at this job.** You may be asked to speak about why you would like this job and about your plans for your life.

▲ **Think about what you would do in the case of a sudden problem.** You may be asked to tell what you would do if a problem happens. Think first about what is safe. Then think about what is right.

OK, go for it! Have a great interview!

What Do You Think?

◈ **Directions:** What are some skills you have? Write them on the lines below.

What I am good at: _____

_____

_____

_____

◈ **Directions:** What jobs would let you use your skills? Write them on the lines below.

Jobs for me: _____

_____

_____

_____

Think About the Story

Use Story Words

◈ **Directions:** Look at your list of story words on page 53. Write a story word on each line.

1. I will _____ for a job at a pet shop.

2. A race car runs _____ a race track.

3. I try to do what is _____.

4. When James was little, he was _____ more shy than he is now.

5. If I got here first, I got here _____ you did.

Remember the Tips

◈ 6. Circle the things you must do when you fill out a job application.

   a. Dress neatly.

   b. Write neatly.

   c. Fill out each line.

   d. Smile as you write, and mean it.

   e. Write in sentences, if you have space.

Your Turn

Directions: Try your hand at filling out a job application. First, write the name of a job you would like to have. Then fill out an application for that job.

Job: _____

Name: _____

Address: _____

_____

_____

Telephone Number: _____

Why I Would Like This Job: _____

_____

_____

_____

_____

_____

Other Jobs I Have Had:

1. _____

2. _____

3. _____

People Who Know Me Well:

	Name	Number
1.	_____	_____
2.	_____	_____
3.	_____	_____

Chapter 1: Summary of Skills and Strategies

Let's look back at what you learned in Chapter 1.

Letters and Sounds

You learned that . . .

- the letters **a, e, i, o,** and **u** are vowels.
- vowels can have a long or a short sound.
- the letter pattern consonant-vowel-consonant-**e,** or CVC**e,** usually stands for a long vowel sound.
- the letter pattern consonant-vowel-consonant, or CVC, usually stands for a short vowel sound.
- the letter **y** can act as a vowel.

Stories and Skills

You learned . . .

- about characters who face problems and find solutions.
- how to apply for a job and go on a job interview.

You learned . . .

- how to use what you know to help you understand stories.
- how to look ahead, or predict, what story characters might do.

Words and Meanings

You learned . . .

- a lot of new words.
- that you can add endings to some words to change their meaning.
- that some words change when you add an ending.
- how to divide a word into syllables.

The chapter review will give you a chance to show what you have learned.

Part A

Summing It Up: Letters and Sounds

▲
▲
- ▶ The letters **a, e, i, o,** and **u** are vowels.
- ▶ A vowel can have a long sound or a short sound.

 Directions: Write each word below in the list where it belongs.

cab	cut	dime
cute	nose	rod
made	net	me
lid		

long vowel	short vowel
1. _____	6. _____
2. _____	7. _____
3. _____	8. _____
4. _____	9. _____
5. _____	10. _____

▲
- ▶ The letters **e, ea,** and **ee** can stand for the long **e** sound.

 Directions: Put a box around each word that has a long **e** sound. Then circle the letter or letters that stand for that sound.

11. beat	14. seed	17. he
12. bet	15. meat	18. met
13. set	16. sell	

> The letter **y** can act as a vowel. It can stand for the long **i** sound or the long **e** sound.

Directions: Write each word below in the list where it belongs.

my	cry	silly
happy	candy	try

y stands for long *e*	*y* stands for long *i*
19. _____	22. _____
20. _____	23. _____
21. _____	24. _____

> ▸ When the same two consonants come together at the end of a word, they stand for one sound.
>
> ▸ When two different consonants come together at the end of a word, they often stand for two sounds.

Directions: Read each word. On the lines below, write 1 or 2 to tell how many consonant sounds you hear at the **end** of each word.

25. fluff _____   28. muss _____

26. desk _____   29. last _____

27. felt _____   30. buzz _____

Directions: Read each word. On the lines below, write 1 or 2 to tell how many consonant sounds you hear in the **middle** of the word.

31. plastic _____   34. very _____

32. after _____   35. skating _____

33. open _____   36. number _____

Part B

Summing It Up: More Word Work

> ▸ Add **s** to make a word tell about more than one thing, or to make it tell about something going on now.
>
> ▸ If a word ends with **x, ch, sh,** or **s,** add **es** instead of **s.**

◆ **Directions:** Add **s** or **es** to each word. Write the new word on the line.

1. loss _____
2. path _____
3. branch _____

4. fish _____
5. mix _____
6. swim _____

> ▸ You can add **ed** or **ing** to many verbs.
>
> ▸ When you add **ed** or **ing** to a verb that ends in **e,** drop the **e.** Then add the ending.
>
> ▸ You can add **ed** or **ing** to a verb with a short vowel that ends in one consonant. Double the last consonant. Then add the ending.

◆ **Directions:** Add **ed** and **ing** to each word below.

	ed	ing
7. frame	_____	_____
8. pop	_____	_____
9. grab	_____	_____
10. mend	_____	_____
11. wish	_____	_____
12. bake	_____	_____

> ▸ Every syllable has a vowel.
>
> ▸ You can split longer words into syllables to help you read them.

Directions: Split the words below into syllables. Write each word. Draw a line in between the two consonants in the middle of the word.

13. brimming _____   16. magnet _____

14. after _____   17. skidding _____

15. mascot _____   18. only_____

Part C

Story Words

Directions: On the lines below, write the word from the list that matches each clue.

open	**year**	**car**
little	**say**	**sentence**
very	**only**	**our**

1. speak _____

2. yours and mine _____

3. not closed _____

4. 365 days _____

5. really, really _____

6. just _____

7. not big _____

8. a string of words _____

9. you ride in this _____

◆ **Directions:** On the lines below, write a word from the list to finish each sentence.

application	new	apply
helmet	interview	give
sound	pocket	grind

10. The _____ of water is nice.

11. My _____ skates fit me fine.

12. I asked my dad to _____ me a ride.

13. I am going to a job _____ at a skate shop.

14. I filled in my job _____.

15. To skate safely, wear a _____.

16. I have a dime in my back _____.

17. The brakes _____. We need new ones.

18. Can I _____ for that job?

◆ **Directions:** Read each word. On the lines below, write a number to tell how many syllables the word has.

19. remember _____   24. know _____

20. woman _____   25. turn _____

21. grind _____   26. after _____

22. great _____   27. before _____

23. along _____   28. right _____

Directions: On the lines below, write the word from the list that matches each clue.

through	push	most	good
school	where	live	work

29. what you do at a job _____

30. place kids go on week days _____

31. in one end and out the other _____

32. word you use to ask about a place _____

33. means "not bad" _____

34. what you do to a kid on a swing _____

35. what you do at home _____

36. not all, but close to all _____

Part D

Think About the Stories

Who Did What?

Directions: This list has the names of the people who were in the stories in Chapter 1. Write a name to answer each question.

Tim	Jade	Mr. Haskins	Jessie
Bob	Mrs. Steed	Don	Travis

1. Who dove deep to get a ring? _____

2. Who helped a kid dive deep? _____

3. Who got a job at a race track? _____

4. Who had some land for a skate place? _____

5. Who let a kid drive a pace car? _____

6. Who helped a pal get a job? _____

7. Who has skated for a year? _____

8. Who is a very good skater? _____

Where Did It Happen?

◆ **Directions:** This list names some spots where the stories took place. Write each place name by the story it goes with.

an empty lot   Chute City Skate Shop
the Stone Hut   a school
a press box   a race track
Red Rocks

Story	Place
9. "The Dive Game" and "Dive Deep"	
10. "A Place to Skate" and "The Skate Ramp"	
11. "Race Track Dreams" and "The Pace Car"	
12. "Skate Shop Job"	

◆

CHAPTER 2

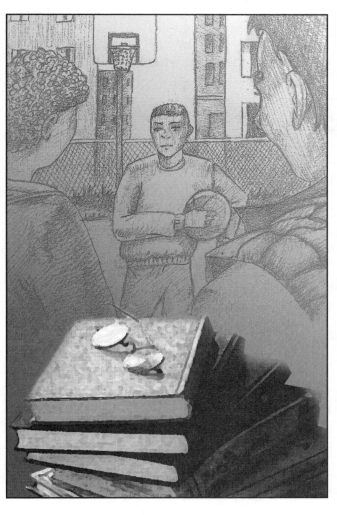

Letters and Sounds

> ▶ The letters **kn** can come at the beginning of a word. They stand for the **n** sound in **not**.
>
> ▶ The letters **wr** can come at the beginning of a word. They stand for the **r** sound in **ran**.

◆ **Directions:** Read each word. Circle the letter or letters that begin the word.

1. know	5. rock	9. wrap
2. wreck	6. wren	10. knot
3. write	7. knife	
4. rude	8. neck	

◆ **Directions:** Now write each word above in the chart where it belongs.

Begins like *net*	Begins like *rim*
11. _____	15. _____
12. _____	16. _____
13. _____	17. _____
14. _____	18. _____
	19. _____
	20. _____

◆ **Directions:** Write the word that fits in each sentence.

21. I did _____ see the magnet.

    knot   **not**   **next**

22. Is this the _____ car?

    right   **write**   **rent**

23. I do not _____ that kid.

    know   **no**   **now**

24. I can _____ the gift.

    rap   **rake**   **wrap**

Word Bank

Write each of these story words in the Word Bank at the back of this book.

Story Words

◆ **Directions:** Read each word to yourself. Then say the word out loud. Write the word on the line. Check the box after each step.

25. too   Read ❑ Say ❑ Write ❑ _____

26. any (a | ny)   Read ❑ Say ❑ Write ❑ _____

27. boy   Read ❑ Say ❑ Write ❑ _____

28. desert (des | ert)   Read ❑ Say ❑ Write ❑ _____

29. hood   Read❑ Say ❑ Write ❑ _____

30. girl   Read ❑ Say ❑ Write ❑ _____

31. ghost   Read ❑ Say ❑ Write ❑ _____

More Word Work

Let's sum up what you know about words and endings.

> ▸ You can add **s** or **es** to many words.
>
> ▸ You can add **ed** or **ing** to many words.
>
> ▸ You can add **ly** to some words.
>
> ▸ Sometimes you have to drop **e** or double the last consonant to add an ending.

◆ **Directions:** Add an ending to each word. Write the new word on the line.

Examples: smug + ly   = smugly
win + ing   = winning
skate + ed = skated

32. swim + ing = _____   **36.** pack + ing = _____

33. race + ed   = _____   **37.** soft + ly   = _____

34. brush + es = _____   **38.** sand + y   = _____

35. swift + ly = _____   **39.** skid + ed   = _____

Use What You Know

What dangers might you face if you drove through a desert? Write what you think on the lines below. Then read this story to find out what happens to three boys who take a desert trip.

_____

_____

THE GIRL IN THE DESERT, PART 1

The day is hot and dry. The sun is blasting with heat. Franky, Riff, and Sly are driving in a lonely desert. Waves of heat rise off the pavement as the day gets late. This trip has lasted for nine days. Sly's old red car has gotten them all the way from the East to the desert. Any day now, the boys will be **wrapping up** this drive. They will be looking at the wide California beaches. And they are happy about it. The desert is so hot! Getting in the water and swimming in those big waves sounds great!

Franky turns up the CD and they all sing along. The time ticks by as the boys look out at the open sky, see the lines on the pavement slide by, and sing. All of a sudden, the car makes a mean sound. It is a very bad grinding sound, too.

"What was that?" yells Riff. He feels a knot in his gut.

Sly goes pale as a ghost. The car comes to a stop, and all is still. Then Sly says, "Man, that sound was not too good. Now the car is stopped. I think we had best get this thing off to the side before any other cars come along. Can you two get out and push?"

Franky and Riff get in back of the old car. The two boys push at the same time. Sly turns the wheel to the right. They push the car to the side, off the pavement. A little oil is dripping from the car.

Sly opens the hood and looks in. "I tell you, man, **you got me.** I do not see any parts missing. I do not know what happened, or what to do."

The boys look each way. They see no cars and no one. All they see is the **vast** desert with its rocks, cliffs, and cactus. "I do not think there are any other people for miles," Franky says.

"This is just great. I mean, now what will we do?" says Riff. "We are stuck in the desert with no car. We do not have much water. We do not have any way to get to a city. What if no one comes by? We can write off getting to the beaches. This hot sun will wipe us out in no time!"

What do you think will happen to the boys in the desert? Write what you think on the lines below. Then read on to find out what happens.

_____

_____

Riff, Sly, and Franky slump down in the shade by the side of the car. No one says a word, but they are all thinking the same thing. It will not be long before the sun goes down. Riff makes knots in a beat up rope. Sly wipes his face. Franky just sits there. They want the mess they are in to be over.

"Your car is an old wreck," gripes Riff. "Why did we bring it?"

Sly looks over at Riff. "At least I have a car! You do not have a car. This car is just fine. It got us this much of the way!"

"Knock it off," Franky says. He knows that this is no time for spats.

All of a sudden, Sly jabs Franky in the ribs. "Would you look at that! What . . . or who . . . is that!? Look! Out over that way!"

Franky and Riff look out at the desert where Sly is looking. Can it be? A kid is coming up to them, out of the desert. It looks like . . . a girl! They are thinking, "Is this for real? The sun and heat have gotten to us. We must not be seeing right. Is this a girl, or is this some ghost?"

As she comes close, they see that her long pants are ripped. Her skin is tan. Her feet are caked with dust. Where could she have come from, on foot like that? The boys did not see any path into the dry hills.

The girl comes up to the car and leans her wrist on the hood. "Say, could you boys use some help?" She gives them a smile. "It looks like your car is going no place fast." She slaps the open hood. "I think I could fix this."

The boys try to speak, but their chins do not move. Then Sly speaks up. "This is a joke, right? This car needs real help, not a desert girl with dust on her feet. Look at you. Where did you come from? No way can you help." ▶

You Be the Judge

◆ 1. Why do the boys think the girl cannot help them? Are the boys right or wrong to think like this?

_____

_____

_____

Think About the Story

Use Story Words

◆ **Directions:** Look at your list of story words on page 69. Write a story word on each line.

2. The kids were driving in the hot _____.

3. The _____ who has a car is named Sly.

4. The boys do not see _____ path leading into the hills.

5. It was dry. It was hot, _____.

6. A dusty _____ came up to the boys.

7. "Is she real, or is she a _____?" they asked.

8. The _____ of the car was up.

When Did It Happen?

◆ 9. Write a number from 1 to 4 in front of each event to show when it happened.

_____ The car makes a grinding sound.

_____ A girl comes out of the desert.

_____ Sly says, "No way can you help."

_____ The kids see oil dripping from the car.

Write Sentences About the Story

◆ **Directions:** Circle the word that best fits in each sentence. Then write the sentence on the line.

10. A girl (come/comes) up to the car.

_____

11. The boys seem to (have/has) no other plans.

_____

How Did They Feel?

◆ **Directions:** On the lines below, write a word from the list to tell how the boys felt.

| shocked | happy | bummed | mad |

12. Riff tells Sly that his car is a wreck. _____

13. The boys see a girl come out of the desert. _____

14. The boys think about swimming in the waves at the beach.
_____

15. The car makes a grinding sound and stops. _____

Words and Meanings

◆ **Directions:** Think about how the **bold** words are used in the story. Then circle the words that show the meaning of each word or phrase.

16. Any day, the boys will be **wrapping up** the ride. This means they will _____.

   a. get going on the next leg of the trip

   b. wrap up the car in red paper

   c. end the trip before long

17. Sly says **"You got me"** when he peeks under the hood. He means _____.

   a. "I do not know what is wrong."

   b. "Let me go!"

   c. "We are stuck here."

18. The boys look out over the **vast** desert. **Vast** must mean _____.

   a. hot and dry

   b. wide and open

   c. little and weak

Look Ahead

◆ **19.** Do you think the odd girl from the desert will help the boys?

_____

_____

Read on to find out.

Letters and Sounds

> ▲
> ▲
> ▲
>
> ▶ The letters **ge** can come at the end of a word. They stand for the **j** sound in **age**.
>
> ▶ The letters **dge** can come at the end of a word. They stand for the **j** sound in **lodge**.

◆ **Directions:** Read each word. Circle **g, ge,** or **dge** at the end of each word.

1. leg	**3.** ledge	**5.** rage	**7.** smudge
2. budge	**4.** huge	**6.** ridge	**8.** fig

◆ **Directions:** Write each word above in the chart where it belongs.

Ends like *pig*	Ends like *age*	Ends like *lodge*
9. _____	11. _____	13. _____
10. _____	12. _____	14. _____
		15. _____
		16. _____

◆ **Directions:** Write the word from the list that finishes each rhyme.

judge   cage   hedge   fig

17. Will a pig eat a _____?

18. Is that a ledge under the _____?

19. I see a smudge on the _____!

20. What is the age of that _____?

Story Words

Directions: Read each word to yourself. Then say the word out loud. Write the word on the line. Check the box after each step.

21. follow (fol | low)   Read ❏ Say ❏ Write ❏ _____

22. want   Read ❏ Say ❏ Write ❏ _____

23. show   Read ❏ Say ❏ Write ❏ _____

24. barefoot (bare | foot) Read ❏ Say ❏ Write ❏ _____

25. under (un | der)   Read ❏ Say ❏ Write ❏ _____

Word Bank

Write each of these story words in the Word Bank at the back of this book.

More Word Work

Directions: Read these sentences.

▸ The car that Sly has is a wreck.

▸ Sly's car is a wreck.

26. What word in the second sentence shows that the car belongs to Sly? Circle the word.

> **TIP:** You can use **'s** to show that a thing belongs to someone.

Directions: Write each sentence again. Use **'s** to show that something belongs to someone.

Example: The bat Rick has is cracked.
   Rick's bat is cracked.

27. The car Jess has is red.

_____

28. The interview Dale had went well.

_____

29. The cap that boy has is neat.

_____

30. The jeans Gwen has are ripped.

_____

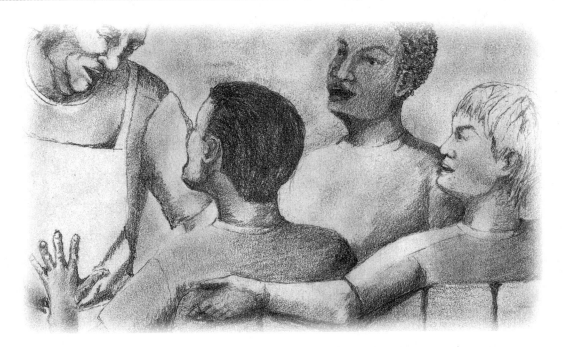

THE GIRL IN THE DESERT, PART 2

Sly, Riff, and Franky look at the smudges on the face of the barefoot girl. Where did she come from? Was she following them? If so, where is her car? She just shows up from **no man's land,** right out of the desert. And what does she mean, she thinks she can fix this car!

She says, "I am not applying for a job. I have no job application. I do not want any interview. Do you want my help or not?"

The boys do not budge. They just look at her, too stunned to say a thing.

The desert girl does not say any more. She just goes to work under the hood of the car. Then she gets down under the car. Some banging sounds come out. After a bit, the barefoot desert girl shows her face. "All right, that wraps it up. Your car is fine now. You can try it."

"I do not think what you did could have helped at all," says Sly. "I think that something very huge is wrong with this car. But OK, I will try." He gets into the car and gives it a try. Sly's car is fine! It runs!

Franky and Riff's faces get red. They know they have judged this girl wrong. She fixed the car. She did know what she was doing! Franky is first to speak. He remembers the mean way they spoke to the girl. "Say, we have to . . . I mean, thank you. That was just great! We did not mean to be rude. What did you say your name is?"

"My name is Ann. Well, I best be going now."

Sly jumps out of the car. He says, "Ann, I want to say thank you, too. I do not know what you did under the hood, but it worked. Say, can we give you a ride? Do you need a lift?"

"No, like I say, I best be going now." Ann turns and sets out the same way that she came. She goes right back out into the desert, as barefoot and dusty as before.

Franky, Sly, and Riff hop back in the car. They look back at Ann. She does not look back. Then they take off, still not knowing what to make of all this. The day is still hot, too. When they come to a **diner,** they stop. They sit down for a bite to eat. They ask the man helping them, "Do you know a girl named Ann who lives out in the desert?"

Do you think the man will know who Ann is? Circle your answer.

YES   NO

Then keep reading to find out.

"Why do you ask, boys?" says the man at the diner.

"Well, our car just broke down out in the desert. This girl named Ann helped us fix it. She was not following us in a car. She did not say much . . . she just came out of the desert, barefoot."

The man gets an odd look on his face. "What's that?" he gulps. "You say her name was Ann and she was barefoot? Where did you say you broke down? Show me the spot on a map."

Sly takes out the map. "Well, it looks like we were about 40 miles to the east. It was right by that ridge, Old Rage Ridge."

"Boys, you may not want to know about this. But I have to tell you. That girl was Barefoot Ann. Her real name is . . . or was . . . Ann Dodge, and she was not following you. Ten years in the past, Ann passed away in the desert. It was right at that same spot you broke down. Her car broke down, and no one stopped to help her. It was hot—really hot. She had no water.

"From time to time, people say, Barefoot Ann comes out of the desert. She shows up only when a car gives out by Old Rage Ridge. It happens the same way each time. She fixes the car. Then she goes right back out to the desert. Yep, boys, looks like the ghost of Barefoot Ann just came along and saved your lives!"

What Do You Think?

◆ 1. Was Barefoot Ann a ghost? Or was the man making up a tale to kid the boys? Could Ann be a real girl who just lives out in the desert? Write what you think on the lines below.

_____

_____

_____

_____

Think About the Story

Use Story Words

◆ **Directions:** Look at your list of story words on page 75. Write a story word on each line.

2. The girl looked _____ the car's hood.

3. Ann was _____, and her feet were caked with dust.

4. The girl did not _____ the boys onto Old Rage Ridge.

5. At first, Sly did not _____ the girl's help.

6. The man asked the kids to _____ him the spot on a map.

Why Did It Happen?

◆ **Directions:** Draw a line from each story event to the reason it happened.

What Happened	Why
7. The man at the diner has an odd look.	○ Ann has fixed the car.
8. Franky's face gets red.	○ The man at the diner wants to see the spot where the car broke down.
9. Sly gets out a map.	○ He knows he was rude to Ann.
10. Franky says, "Thank you."	○ The boys say they met a barefoot girl named Ann.

Write Sentences About the Story

◆ **Directions:** Use words from the story to answer these questions.

11. Why were the boys stunned when Ann showed up?

_____

_____

12. What does the man say about why Ann fixes cars on Old Rage Ridge?

_____

_____

The Big Idea

◆ 13. What sentence best sums up the end of this story? Circle that sentence.

    a. The boys go to a diner for a good meal.

    b. A man tells the boys who Ann is, and why she helped them.

    c. Now that the car is fixed, the trip goes on.

Words and Meanings

◆ **Directions:** Think about how the **bold** words are used in the story. Then circle the words that show the meaning of each word or phrase.

14. In the story, **no man's land** means _____.

    a. land that a man will not sell

    b. land that no one wants

    c. land that is empty of people

15. In this story, a **diner** is _____.

    a. a place to eat

    b. a person who eats out

    c. a meal on a plate

Letters and Sounds

> **△ △ △ ▶ TIP:** ▶ The letters **th, sh, ch,** and **wh** come at the beginning of some words. They stand for one sound.
>
> ▶ The letters **th, sh, ch,** and **tch** come at the end of some words. They stand for one sound.

◆ **Directions:** Read these words. Circle **th, sh, ch, wh,** or **tch.**

1. thin	6. which	11. rich
2. thick	7. wheel	12. such
3. sheep	8. wrath	13. pitch
4. chat	9. with	14. ditch
5. chin	10. push	

◆ **Directions:** Now write each word above in the chart where it belongs.

Begins like . . . *thing*	*show*	*chick*	*what*
15. _____ 16. _____	17. _____	18. _____ 19. _____	20. _____ 21. _____
Ends like . . . *path*	*dish*	*much*	*clutch*
22. _____ 23. _____	24. _____	25. _____ 26. _____ 27. _____	28. _____ 29. _____

◆ **Directions:** Write a word from the list to finish each sentence.

shines	chat	thick	wheels
ditch	thin	path	wish

30. A snake is _____.
31. A log is _____.
32. Hike on a _____.
33. Dig a _____.
34. The sun _____.
35. Pals like to _____.
36. A car has _____.
37. Make a _____.

Story Words

Word Bank

Write each of these story words in the Word Bank at the back of this book.

◆ **Directions:** Read each word to yourself. Then say the word out loud. Write the word on the line. Check the box after each step.

38. also (al | so)   Read ❑ Say ❑ Write ❑ _____

39. around (a | round)   Read ❑ Say ❑ Write ❑ _____

40. area (ar | e | a)   Read ❑ Say ❑ Write ❑ _____

41. alien (a | li | en) Read ❑ Say ❑ Write ❑ _____

42. gold   Read ❑ Say ❑ Write ❑ _____

More Word Work

You know how to split words like **magnet** and **mapping** into syllables:

mag | net   map | ping

You split them in between the two consonants. But how do you split a word like **wishes** or **ditches** into syllables? Here's how:

wish | es   ditch | es

▶ **TIP:** When the letters **th, sh, ch,** and **tch** stand for one sound in a word, those letters stay together when you split the word into syllables.

◆ **Directions:** Circle the letters **th, sh, ch,** or **tch** in each word. Then write the word. Draw a line to split it into syllables.

Example: ditches   ditch | es

43. patches   _____

44. riches   _____

45. pitching   _____

46. pushing   _____

47. Dutchman   _____

48. hatchling _____

49. teething   _____

Sign outside of Area 51

TALES FROM THE DESERT

Part 1: Area 51

What the Air Force Says. The desert is a rich place for UFO tales. Out in Nevada, more than 100 miles from Las Vegas, is a place with the name "Area 51." Area 51 is a block of desert land. A U.S. Air Force base and some dry **lake beds** are inside Area 51. The Air Force keeps all people out of this area. No one can go into Area 51 to look around. If people show up on any part of Area 51, they can be locked up. Why is the place closed to people? What is going on at Area 51?

The air base is a place where new U.S. spy planes are tested. At least, that is what the U.S. Air Force says.

What Others Think. Some people think that alien space ships are also kept at Area 51. They say that aliens are working with the Air Force there. They are teaching the Air Force how to make planes that fly like UFOs. Some say that alien space ships are kept under the desert in huge tunnels. Others say that the alien craft are kept in tunnels inside a ridge line of hills that runs through one of the dry lakes.

Many people drive out to the desert by Area 51 to try to see what is going on there. They stop in the hot, dry desert heat and look around. They look for alien space ships in the sky. They look for hints of aliens on the desert land.

What do you think? Are space aliens for real? Are the tales fact, or not?

What other odd tales have come out of the desert?
Read Part 2 to find out.

Part 2: Lost Gold Mines

The Lost Dutchman Mine. What if you could find gold around or under the hills of the desert? Many, many people have dreamed of it. And many go out into the desert wishing to find gold and lost mines.

Out in Arizona, tales of gold and lost mines have been around for more than 100 years. The ones about the Lost Dutchman Mine may be the most chilling. It seems that in the 1840s, three men of the Peralta clan of Mexico came across a very rich **seam of gold** in the Superstition Mountains. They made many trips to the mine, taking gold back to their homes. But then, in 1848, Apaches went after the Peraltas and killed some of them. The Apaches were mad that gold was being taken from their land. An Apache woman, or maybe more, hid the seams of gold with dust or rocks.

The mine was lost for more than 20 years.

The Peraltas Come Back. Then Ramon Peralta, who had not been killed, went back to Arizona. His plan was to find the mine one more time, and he did. Two pals were with him. They were so happy that they told a man they met in the hills about the mine. That was not good thinking. The old man, a Dutchman named Jacob Walzer, killed them. From then on, Walzer was the only one who knew where the mine was. He got very rich and went to live in a very nice home in the desert.

Before he passed away, he told a woman and a man where the mine was. He even gave them maps. But they could not find the mine. Others went to the Superstition Mountains to look for the Lost Dutchman Mine. No one could find it. More than 20 people lost their lives trying. Some say the Apaches cast a spell on the mine. But people still look for the mine. Why? It may have $100,000,000 in gold still in it!

A Stone Map. In 1952, some people driving through Arizona stopped to get out and stretch. The man driving stepped out on the desert. He saw something that looked like part of a brick sticking up. He dug it up. It was not a brick, but a stone. Some Spanish writing and other lines were **etched** into the stone. Some chipped lines on the stone looked like a girl with a hat on. Other lines on the map were in the shape of a cross. The map had numbers on it, too. Was it an old map? What did the numbers and lines mean? The man followed the etchings on the map. The etchings told him to go 18 steps this way, then go that way, and so on. In doing so, he turned up other stone maps. These may show the way to the Lost Dutchman Mine. But they still have not helped anyone find the path to the big seam of gold.

Two stone maps

What Do You Think?

 1. Is Area 51 home to alien space ships? Or is it really just a place for the U.S. to test spy planes? Write what you think on the lines below.

_____

_____

2. Do lost mines still rest under the desert sand? If so, will people find them one of these days?

_____

_____

Think About the Story

Use Story Words

 Directions: Look at your list of story words on page 81. Write a story word on each line.

3. An _____ is a being from space.

4. You would be rich if you had a _____ mine.

5. The word _____ means "and."

6. A race car goes _____ a track.

7. An _____ is a big space or a bit of land.

The Big Idea

8. Which sentence best sums up what "Tales from the Desert" is all about? Circle that sentence and write it on the lines.

    a. There are lots of odd tales about the desert, and people do not know which ones are for real.

    b. The desert is filled with gold miners and aliens, and most of them make maps.

    c. People can go to the desert to find out what is real and what is not.

_____

_____

_____

When Did It Happen?

◆ **9.** Write a number from 1 to 4 in front of each event to show when it happened.

_____ A driver dug up a stone map in the desert.

_____ Jacob Walzer dug gold in the desert.

_____ Walzer gave maps to a man and a woman.

_____ Other stone maps were dug up.

What Are the Facts?

◆ **Directions:** Write **T** next to the sentences that say true things about Area 51. Write **F** next to the sentences that do not.

10. _____ It has a ridge of hills that runs through a dry lake.

11. _____ It is a place where anyone can go.

12. _____ It is in Nevada.

13. _____ It is about 600 miles from Las Vegas.

14. _____ The U.S. Air Force runs it.

15. _____ It has a diner just for aliens.

Words and Meanings

◆ **Directions:** Think about how the **bold** words are used in the story. Then circle the words that show the meaning of each word or phrase.

16. A **seam of gold** is _____.
   a. gold to knit with
   b. a thin pipe for bringing gold out of the mine
   c. a long strip of gold between rocks

17. To **etch** a line into stone is to _____.
   a. dig into the stone using a knife or blade
   b. write on the stone using a pen
   c. find a line that is there

18. A **lake bed** is _____.
   a. the peaks around a lake
   b. the shape of the land under a lake
   c. a place for a lake to sleep

Letters and Sounds

◆ **Directions:** You know the words **for** and **more**. Write **for** and **more** on the lines. Then circle the letters **or** in each word.

1. for _____

2. more _____

If you can read **for** and **more**, you can read many words with **or**. Read these words.

    bore   **corn**   **storm**   **wore**   **short**

◆ **Directions:** The letters **or** stand for the same sound in each word. Write the words below on the lines. Circle the letter pattern **or**.

3. bore _____   7. boring _____

4. corn _____   8. corny _____

5. storm _____   9. storming _____

6. store _____   10. stored _____

TIP: ▶ When **o** is followed by **r,** the **o** stands for a sound that is not long or short.

    ▶ The letters **or** and **ore** stand for the **or** sound in **for** and **more**.

◆ **Directions:** See how many words you can make. Write the letters on the lines.

t	m	w	b	c	st

11. _____ orn   15. _____ ore

12. _____ orn   16. _____ ore

13. _____ orn   17. _____ ore

14. _____ orn   18. _____ ore

Story Words

Word Bank

Write each of these story words in the Word Bank at the back of this book.

◆ **Directions:** Read each word to yourself. Then say the word out loud. Write the word on the line. Check the box after each step.

19. three   Read ❑ Say ❑ Write ❑ _____

20. small   Read ❑ Say ❑ Write ❑ _____

21. put   Read ❑ Say ❑ Write ❑ _____

22. rubber (rub | ber)   Read ❑ Say ❑ Write ❑ _____

23. fashion (fash | ion) Read ❑ Say ❑ Write ❑ _____

More Word Work

◆ **Directions:** The words below are made up of words and endings. Read each word. Then write the word and the ending that was added to it.

Examples: stored   store + ed

coring   core + ing

shortly   short + ly

24. stores   _____ + _____

25. boring   _____ + _____

26. stormed   _____ + _____

27. shorts   _____ + _____

28. storing   _____ + _____

◆ **Directions:** Write each word again. Draw a line to split it into syllables.

Example: boring   bor | ing

29. storing   _____

30. story   _____

31. shortly   _____

> **TIP:** When you split a word with the vowel plus **r** sound into syllables, the vowel and the **r** always stay together.

Use What You Know

What kinds of small businesses can people start on their own? Write your answers on the lines below. Then read the next story to find out about a woman who turned a fun idea into a fashion trend!

_____

_____

_____

STRETCHING THE LIMITS, PART 1

Meet Ave Green. For Ave, a small **whim** turned into a big deal. The big deal is rubber bands! Ave's rubber bands, though, are not just any rubber bands. They are fashion bands. People put them right around their wrists. The bands may be worn as rings. Very thick, big rubber bands can be used to wrap gift boxes.

Ave Green

You may be asking, What is so great about a rubber band, that boring little thing that any one can find in most desks? How can a rubber band be a fashion trend?

Ave Green's life story is a tale of three cities. She was born in the Chicago area. Then she made St. Paul, Minnesota, her home for 10 years. After that, Ave went out to Los Angeles. She worked in L.A. for a few years. She acted in TV ads and in some films. Ave liked acting, and it was going along well. Still, she wanted to apply her skills to more than just acting. One day, Ave went back to St. Paul. On the way, she saw some one who had on a rubber band. The rubber band had words printed on it.

This small fact stuck with Ave. She turned it over and over, thinking about rubber bands with writing on them. On a whim, she looked into it more. In fact, she put in a lot of time finding out more about rubber bands.

She looked into the cost of getting rubber bands in many sizes—big and small, thick and thin. She asked what it would cost to put **printed words** on the rubber bands. She looked into what shades she could get the bands in—red, black, white, pink, green, and other shades. She asked what shades of ink could be used for printing on the bands. Ave also went to stores to see if, or where, people were selling rubber bands like those.

Ave felt that it would be a **snap** to make and sell batches of neat rubber bands. These rubber bands would have fun words and sayings printed on them. Three sets of fashion rubber bands would be the core of what Ave would make. One set could be worn on the wrist. One set was made to be worn as rings. The last set was a "big band" set for wrapping boxes and putting around things. All the bands were to have cute, funny, or wise sayings on them.

Ave chose some sayings to be printed on the rubber bands. Some of the sayings were just one, two, or three words. Others were short sentences. These are some of the sayings Ave chose to put on her wrist bands:

▲ Life is sweet.

▲ Snap out of it!

The ring bands were small. Ave planned for the ring bands to have just one or two words, such as:

▲ Trust

▲ Hope

▲ Peace

▲ Go, Girl! ▶

Some of Ave Green's bands

What Do You Think?

◆ 1. Do you like Ave's rubber band fashion? Would you get some if you could? Write what you think on the lines below.

_____

_____

◆ 2. What if you could put a saying or a word on a fashion band? What would you put there? Write your idea in the box.

```
┌─────────────────────────────────────────────┐
│                                             │
│                                             │
│                                             │
│                                             │
└─────────────────────────────────────────────┘
```

Think About the Story

Use Story Words

◆ **Directions:** Look at your list of story words on page 87. Write a story word on each line.

3. This stuff is stretchy. _____

4. One and one and one add up to this. _____

5. This means "little." _____

6. This means "to place" or "to set down." _____

7. If how you look means a lot to you, you are into this.

_____

Write Sentences About the Story

◆ **Directions:** Use words from the story to answer these questions.

8. Where was Ave Green born?

_____

9. How did she first think of rubber bands as a fashion?

_____

10. What did Ave need to find out before she got going with her plan?

_____

_____

11. What did she plan to put on the ring bands?

_____

_____

What Are the Facts?

◆ **Directions:** Put a **T** next to the sentences that tell about Ave Green and her fashion bands. Put an **F** next to the sentences that do not.

12. _____ Some fashion bands are worn around the neck.

13. _____ Some fashion bands can make gifts look great.

14. _____ Ave was born in L.A.

15. _____ Ave spent more than 10 years in St. Paul.

16. _____ Ave planned to make three sizes of rubber bands for her first line of fashion bands.

Words and Meanings

◆ **Directions:** Think about how the **bold** words are used in the story. Then circle the words that show the meaning of each word or phrase.

17. What is a **whim**?
    a. a plan that is all worked out
    b. something fun that you just think of
    c. a rubber band with words printed on it

18. In this story, **printed words** are _____.
    a. words stamped on with ink
    b. words printed on with a pen
    c. words you see in a story

19. Ave felt it would be a **snap** to make and sell the fashion bands. Here, **snap** means _____.
    a. a stinging slap
    b. the sound a twig makes when you step on it
    c. an easy task

Look Ahead

◆ **20.** Do you think people will like Ave's fashion bands? Will she get to sell them? Write what you think on the lines below. Then read the rest of the story to find out.

_____

_____

Letters and Sounds

◆ **Directions:** You know the word **her**. Write **her** on the line. Then circle the letters **er**.

1. her _____

The word **bird** has the same vowel plus **r** sound as **her**. Write **bird**. Circle the letters **ir**.

2. bird _____

▲
▲
▲ **TIP:** ▶ When **e** or **i** is followed by **r**, the **e** or **i** stands for a sound that is not long or short.
　　　　 ▶ The letters **er** and **ir** can stand for the vowel plus **r** sound in **her**.

◆ **Directions:** Write the words below on the lines. Circle the letter pattern **er** or **ir**.

3. letter _____   7. lettering _____

4. fir _____   8. firs _____

5. stir _____   9. stirring _____

6. fern _____   10. ferns _____

◆ **Directions:** Write each word below where it belongs in the chart.

　　　　bend　　　　whir　　　　ripped
　　　　herd　　　　rent　　　　stern

short *i* sound	vowel plus *r* sound in *her*	short *e* sound
11. _____	12. _____	15. _____
	13. _____	16. _____
	14. _____	

Story Words

◆ **Directions:** Read each word to yourself. Then say the word out loud. Write the word on the line. Check the box after each step.

17. does   Read ❑ Say ❑ Write ❑ _____

18. another (a | noth | er) Read ❑ Say ❑ Write ❑ _____

19. large   Read ❑ Say ❑ Write ❑ _____

20. friend   Read ❑ Say ❑ Write ❑ _____

21. style   Read ❑ Say ❑ Write ❑ _____

More Word Work

◆ **22.** Read these sentences. Circle the **bold** word that names a person.

▸ They did a lot of **work** on that house.

▸ There was a **worker** over there all the time.

23. What ending was added to the word **work**? _____
A worker is one who works.

> **TIP:** The ending **er** can mean "one who." You can add **er** to some words to make them tell about someone who does something.

◆ **Directions:** Add **er** to each word. Write the word in the sentence.

Examples: bake → The baker made some sweet treats.
win → The winner got a new bike.

24. swim → Which _____ crossed the finish line first?

25. hike → Do you see a _____ on the path?

26. interview → The _____ asked me what jobs I have had.

27. sell → The _____ of the car wants cash.

> **Remember!** When you add an ending like **er** to a word that ends in **e,** drop the **e.** Then add the ending. If the word has a short vowel sound and ends with one consonant, double the consonant. Then add the ending.

STRETCHING THE LIMITS, PART 2

Ave Green has this to say about how she turned into a maker and seller of fashion rubber bands: "I followed a whim that I had this inkling about—so I made them!" She did her home work. She asked her friends if they would like fashion rubber bands. She felt that rubber bands were a **fad** that was going to catch on big. She liked taking a small thing, **putting a spin** on it, making it seem new. It was time to give the rubber band some style! So Ave went for it.

She opened up shop, ordering and selling the rubber bands from her home. Before the end of 1998, Ave was taking her rubber bands around to stores in the area.

Shops picked up Ave's rubber bands. Now they are selling in many stores around the United States. Shoppers liked the bands, and a style trend began to take off. Then the bands showed up in large stores.

Some of Ave's best sales have come from sports people. Some top NBA **dudes** sport them. Kevin Garnett, of the Minnesota Timberwolves team, has worn rubber bands on his wrists for years. Now he puts on Ave's rubber bands. Garnett and the U.S. Dream Team wore the bands at the 2000 Olympics in Australia. The bands said, "Dream Team 2000: Nothing Less Than Gold."

Lamar Odom of the L.A. Clippers and Stephon Marbury of the New Jersey Nets have worn the bands. CD maker Jimmy Jam gives them out as gifts. He can be seen with them on his wrist for luck. He showed them to singer Janet Jackson. She likes them, too. Bill Clinton, Jesse Ventura, and Michael Jordan have also worn the bands.

Does Ave think her rubber bands will keep selling well? She thinks it is a good bet. "After all," says Ave, "they are fun. And a rubber band is a thing you use! They are in every home. They are in most stores. If the printing does get worn off, you will still use the rubber band." Ave wants to make more rubber band styles.

This page shows more of Ave's three rubber band styles and their sayings. One band in each set is a blank form. The blank ones are for you. Think of fun sayings that could be printed in the blanks. Think of sayings that would work for many people.

You Be the Judge

◆ **Directions:** What does it take to turn a whim into a real plan that works? List three things you must have or do in order to do this.

1. _____

2. _____

3. _____

Think About the Story

Use Story Words

◆ **Directions:** Look at your list of story words on page 93. Write a story word on each line.

4. This has to do with fashion. _____

5. This is a form of the word **do.** _____

6. This means "one more." _____

7. This is a word for one you are close to. _____

8. This means "big." _____

When Did It Happen?

◆ 9. Write a number from 1 to 4 in front of each event to show when it happened.

_____ Ave moved to L.A.

_____ Ave asked friends if they would like fashion bands.

_____ Ave's fashion bands made their way to stores all over the U.S.

_____ Ave looked into the cost of having rubber bands made.

Write Sentences About the Story

◆ **Directions:** Circle the word that best fits each sentence. Then write that sentence on the line.

10. Some people (order/orders) large numbers of the bands.

_____

11. Lamar Odom and Stephon Marbury (wear/wears) Ave's bands.

_____

12. Ave (like/likes) giving a little thing like a rubber band a bit of style.

_____

Words and Meanings

◆ **Directions:** Think about how the **bold** words are used in the story. Then circle the words that show the meaning of each word or phrase.

13. A **fad** is _____.
    a. a rubber band with letters on it
    b. another word for "fun"
    c. a trend that takes off fast

14. To **put a spin** on something is to _____.
    a. turn it around and around
    b. use it or think of it in a new way
    c. put a cloth on top of it

15. NBA dudes **sport** the bands. This means they _____.
    a. pitch them into the basket
    b. put them on for fashion
    c. help Ave sell them

The Big Idea

◆ 16. Which sentence best sums up what the whole story is about? Circle it.
    a. A woman named Ave Green turned a whim into a big biz through hard work and good thinking.
    b. NBA dudes made a new fashion trend by sporting Ave Green's rubber bands.
    c. If you fail at first, just keep on trying.

Think About It

◆ 17. What do you think the name of the story, "Stretching the Limits," means? Write what you think on the lines below.

_____

_____

_____

_____

Letters and Sounds

◆ **Directions:** You know the word **car.** Write **car** on the line. Circle the letters **ar.**

1. car _____

If you can read **car,** you can read many words with **ar.** Read these words.

start	**art**	**far**	**star**

◆ **Directions:** The letters **ar** stand for the same sound in each word. Write the words below on the lines. Circle the letter pattern **ar** in each word.

2. farm   _____   6. farmer   _____

3. part   _____   7. parting   _____

4. park   _____   8. parking   _____

5. chart   _____   9. charted   _____

TIP: ▶ When **a** is followed by **r,** the **a** stands for a sound that is not long or short.

▶ The letters **ar** stand for the **ar** sound in **car.**

◆ **Directions:** Write the letters on the lines. See how many words you can make.

b	c	d	st	m	p	t	j

10. _____ ar   14. _____ art

11. _____ ar   15. _____ art

12. _____ ar   16. _____ art

13. _____ ar   17. _____ art

Story Words

◆ **Directions:** Read each word to yourself. Then say the word out loud. Write the word on the line. Check the box after each step.

Word Bank

Write each of these story words in the Word Bank at the back of this book.

18. even (e | ven)   Read ❑ Say ❑ Write ❑ _____

19. because (be | cause) Read ❑ Say ❑ Write ❑ _____

20. here   Read ❑ Say ❑ Write ❑ _____

21. basketball   Read ❑ Say ❑ Write ❑ _____
    (bas | ket | ball)

22. court   Read ❑ Say ❑ Write ❑ _____

23. play   Read ❑ Say ❑ Write ❑ _____

24. surprise (sur | prise) Read ❑ Say ❑ Write ❑ _____

More Word Work

▶ **Remember:** You have learned that you can add **'s** to a word to show that something belongs to someone.

▶ **TIP:**   You can also add **'s** to words that name places and things.

◆ **Directions:** Write each sentence again. Use **'s** to show that something belongs to a person, place, or thing.

Example: The lot the city has is empty now.
                The city's lot is empty now.

25. The players the team has are good!

_____

26. The courts the park has are not well lit.

_____

27. The crops of the farmer are ripe.

_____

28. The lock on that bike needs oil.

_____

Use What You Know

The next story is about a short kid named Jamal who wants to play on a basketball team. What problems do you think Jamal will face? Write your answers on the lines below. Then read the story to find out if Jamal makes the team.

_____

_____

_____

THE SURPRISE STAR, PART 1

Jamal sped around the corner at a flat out run. He grasped his basketball in one arm. It was 4:00, time for the after school pick up game at the park basketball courts. This week, teams were forming for the city basketball contest. Jamal was in a rush because he did not want to miss getting on a team. It was a freezing day. He wrapped his scarf more snugly to keep the brisk winter air off his neck. Then he pumped his short legs even faster. His 5'3" body zipped down the street.

Three boys were on the court when he charged up. They were tossing up shots, passing, and blocking out under one of the baskets. One of them snatched the ball, turned, and leaped into the air. He held the ball up. Then he slammed it down through the basket. He made it look easy.

Jamal darted up to the basket at the other end of the court. He leaped to jam one through in the same fashion. It was no use. He could not dunk. His short legs hardly got off the court. His shot was lame. The ball missed. The other three boys stopped their play. They turned to look over at Jamal as if he were an alien being.

"What does that short kid think he is doing out here?" one of them asked the others.

"Did someone say that fleas could try out for the basketball teams?" said another. "But then, even a flea can make a better shot than that kid."

"What was that shot, Shorty? You missed!" the other boy piped in.

Jamal was **steamed** at these jokes about his small size. But he did not let it show. "I am all set to play here," he said, putting his ball down at the side of the court. He went over to the larger boys. "I want to be on a team because I can play this game. I can play it well, even if I am not as big as you."

"All right, Flea-Boy, we will see what you can do," said the largest of the three other boys. "I'm Tyrell. This is Carlos. That is Marcus. We will go two on two. Here, you and Carlos will take on Marcus and me, OK? But I will tell you one thing. Just because you are short, do not think we are going to be easy on you."

Do you think the others will let Jamal be on a team with them?

Circle your answer.   YES   NO

Keep reading to find out if Jamal can play basketball as well as he says he can.

"Be as hard on me as you want," said Jamal. "I can play with you. Just try to get by me. You may be larger, Tyrell, but I am faster—a lot faster. I will **pester** you so bad! You will see. You will not get one good shot off!"

The three large boys looked at each other and smiled. They did not think much of this smaller kid. Just then, Jamal dodged fast through them, snatching the ball from Tyrell. The game was on! Marcus ran under the basket and waved his hand at Jamal. Jamal was a great dribbler! He faked Tyrell and whizzed past him, right under his nose. Then he whipped a pass to Marcus, who jammed the ball through for a basket. Both Tyrell and Carlos looked surprised.

The game went on that way. Time after time, play after play, Jamal was in the thick of things. He seemed not to get tired. Every time Carlos or Tyrell had the ball, Jamal was there poking it away. He zipped around like a pesky fly. They could not get free for a good shot. They could not even make a good pass because of the **fleet** little pest!

When at last they stopped for a rest, Tyrell had a wry smile on his face. "Flea-Boy, you surprised us big time! You may be short, but you are a real player! You are like a rubber ball out on the court, pinging all over the place. I think you will be a great part of our team."

"Speaking of that," said Carlos, "before it gets dark, we just have time to go get on the roster for the city teams." ▶

You Be the Judge

◆ 1. Do you think it is OK to judge people by the way they look? Why or why not? Write what you think on the lines below.

_____

_____

2. Think of a time when you judged someone by looks only, and it turned out you were wrong. What happened?

_____

_____

Think About the Story

Use Story Words

◆ **Directions:** Look at your list of story words on page 99. Write a story word on each line.

3. A _____ is something you do not expect.

4. One sport lots of people like is _____.

5. There are two baskets on a basketball _____.

6. 2, 4, 6, and 8 are _____ numbers.

7. This word is used to tell why. The word is _____.

8. When you take part in a game, you _____.

9. The word _____ means "in this place."

Why Did It Happen?

◆ **Directions:** Draw a line from each story event to the reason it happened.

What Happened	Why
10. Jamal sped to the court as fast as he could.	○ The players made fun of his small size.
11. Jamal was mad at the other three players at first.	○ Jamal had shown him that he was a good basketball player.
12. Tyrell had to smile at Jamal.	○ Jamal was all over the other players.
13. Tyrell tells Jamal he is "pesky."	○ He did not want to miss getting on the team.

The Big Idea

◆ **14.** What sentence best sums up the story so far? Circle that sentence.
  a. A big kid finds out that you do not have to be big to be a star.
  b. A short kid proves that he is a good basketball player.
  c. City kids are forming teams for a basketball contest.

Write Sentences About the Story

◆ **Directions:** Use words from the story to answer these questions.

15. What names do the kids call Jamal? Why?

_____

_____

16. How does Jamal prove that he can play?

_____

_____

17. How do you know that the three bigger kids want Jamal on their team?

_____

_____

Words and Meanings

◆ **Directions:** Think about how the **bold** words are used in the story. Then circle the words that show the meaning of each word or phrase.

18. A **fleet** little pest is a _____.
  a. fast little pest
  b. smart little pest
  c. odd little pest

19. Jamal was **steamed** about the jokes. Here, **steamed** means _____.
  a. sad and lonely
  b. mad as can be
  c. put into a pot of water

20. To **pester** people means to _____.
  a. bother them over and over
  b. toss bugs at them
  c. make shots over them

Letters and Sounds

These consonants often come together at the end of a word:

nk	**ng**	**nd**	**nt**

◆ **Directions:** Read these words. Circle the two consonants at the end of each word.

1. pink   2. sing   3. sand   4. lint

◆ **Directions:** Sometimes these consonants come together in the middle of a word. Write each word. Circle **nk, ng, nd,** or **nt.**

5. winter _____   8. thinking _____

6. stinger _____   9. blinkers _____

7. findings _____   10. swinging _____

▲ ▲ ▲   **TIP:** ▸ The letters **nk** stand for one sound—the sound you hear at the end of **pink.**

▸ The letters **ng** stand for one sound—the sound you hear at the end of **sing.**

◆ **Directions:** Write the letters on the lines. See how many words you can make.

st	bl	br	th	p	wr	s	l

11. _____ ink   15. _____ ong   19. _____ and

12. _____ ink   16. _____ ong   20. _____ and

13. _____ ink   17. _____ ong   21. _____ and

14. _____ ink   18. _____ ong   22. _____ and

Word Bank

Write each of these story words in the Word Bank at the back of this book.

Story Words

 **Directions:** Read each word to yourself. Then say the word out loud. Write the word on the line. Check the box after each step.

23. move   Read ❑ Say ❑ Write ❑ _____

24. kind   Read ❑ Say ❑ Write ❑ _____

25. shoot   Read ❑ Say ❑ Write ❑ _____

26. prove   Read ❑ Say ❑ Write ❑ _____

More Word Work

Directions: Add an ending to each word below. Pick the ending from the list. Use each ending at least one time.

ed	ing	s
ly	er	es

27. thank _____

28. bank _____

29. sting _____

30. stand _____

31. box _____

32. sharp _____

33. wise _____

34. farm _____

35. rent _____

36. wish _____

Directions: Read each word. Then write the word and the ending that was added to it.

Example: stretched   stretch + ed

37. mover _____ + _____

38. kindly _____ + _____

39. following _____ + _____

40. cheaply _____ + _____

41. diner _____ + _____

THE SURPRISE STAR, PART 2

The name of the team started by Tyrell, Carlos, Marcus, and Jamal was the Rockets. Being on the team was not so easy for Jamal at first. Some people on the team did not want him to play. At 5'3" tall, Jamal was shorter than any other player on any of the city's teams. They felt he was too small to make shots and stop other players. But Jamal just kept showing up and playing his best. Time after time Jamal proved his skill and drive. This changed things in a big way. The big men on the team were great shooters. They could stretch up, slam dunk, and bat the other team's shots into the stands. They each had great moves. But in a way, it was Jamal who pulled them all into form.

Jamal had great skill as a team player. He was a born leader. He had a good sense of where each player needed to be at all times. Also, he played smart from start to end. Yes, he could run rings around the other players. Yes, he never seemed to run out of steam. But when the chips were down, he never made a bad move. The Rockets also liked Jamal because he helped other players look good. He would swipe the ball from the other team and move with it. In a wink he would get the ball to one of the larger kids, who would then shoot and score. He got the name "Master Passer" because he hardly ever missed his mark. And because of his speed, the whole pace of the team's game picked up. Things just happened faster.

The Rockets beat team after team. One day, Jamal was on TV. Basketball fans around the city got to know about Jamal, the short basketball player with the great hands and the jet speed. Some people started coming out to the games just to see him play.

After some time, the play-offs started. Now the whole city would find out who was best. First three, then two, then only one more game was left to play. The Rockets had made it to the big game.

Do you think Jamal's team, the Rockets, will win the play-offs? Circle your answer.

YES   NO

Then read on to find out if the Rockets win the play-offs.

The Rockets had the ball. Tyrell, the best big man, ran down the court, and Jamal passed him the ball. The score was even, and things were happening fast. The clock was running down, and the end of the game was close. But Tyrell stepped on the end line! The ball went to the other team, the Stars.

A Stars player tossed the ball in from the side. The Stars pushed on to their basket, working the ball back and forth. Jamal, as ever, played smart. He cut off the path to the basket. Then he moved so fast that he seemed to be in three places at a time. He was over here, and here, and here. He kept blocking the way, keeping his hand in the face of the player with the ball. Then, fast as a blink, things changed. Jamal grabbed the ball in mid-air.

The fans were on their feet, yelling at the tops of their lungs. The small man, the Master Passer, had the ball! Spinning around, Jamal sped for his team's basket. His team was right with him. **Faking a pass** to Tyrell on his left, he whipped the ball to Carlos. Carlos snatched it and stopped on a dime. He had only **three ticks** left to make his shot. He leaped up. At the top of his jump, he let the ball go.

The ball hit the back rim of the basket, went up, came down, and hit the rim another time. Then, get this: The ball kind of hung on the rim, or seemed to, for a very long time. The people in the stands were going nuts. Both teams looked on while the clock ran out. The buzzer blasted the air. And . . . the ball fell . . . in!

The Rockets were the city-wide **champs.** The team mobbed Carlos in a huge pile up. Then Carlos broke free and grabbed Jamal. "Flea-Boy, we did it!" Carlos yelled. He got down on one leg and they both held up their arms. They were winners! The whole city knew it! Then the team lifted Jamal, the short one, up in the air.

◆

You Be the Judge

◆ 1. What do you think was the best thing about the way Jamal played? Why? Write what you think on the lines below.

_____

_____

Think About the Story

Use Story Words

◆ **Directions:** Look at your list of story words on page 105. Write a story word on each line.

2. Jamal had to _____ that he could play.

3. If you do not stay in one place, you _____.

4. One meaning for the word _____ is "very nice to others."

5. When you _____ a basketball, you try to get it into the basket.

The Big Idea

◆ 6. What does this story prove? Circle the sentence that best sums up what the story shows.

   a. Size is not the only thing that matters in basketball.

   b. The larger the better, if you want to play sports.

   c. Basketball is a good game for people of all ages and sizes.

Why Did It Happen?

◆ **Directions:** Draw a line from each story event to the reason it happened.

What Happened	Why
7. Jamal had a hard time on the team at first.	○ Jamal was fast, and he kept the players running.
8. The pace of the game picked up when Jamal was on the court.	○ The Rockets were the winners.
9. Carlos yelled, "Flea-Boy, we did it!"	○ Jamal passed the ball to Carlos.
10. Carlos made the winning shot.	○ The other players did not want Jamal to play.

Write Sentences About the Story

◆ **Directions:** Use words from the story to answer these questions.

11. What team was the winner?

_____

12. What was the name of the team that did not win?

_____

13. What was different about Jamal, other than his size?

_____

_____

14. How did the Rockets feel about Jamal at the end? How do you know?

_____

_____

Words and Meanings

◆ **Directions:** Think about how the **bold** words are used in the story. Then circle the words that show the meaning of each word or phrase.

15. **Three ticks** means _____.
    a. some nasty bugs
    b. a long stretch of time
    c. three seconds

16. **Champs** are _____.
    a. winners
    b. chomping teeth
    c. apes

17. To **fake a pass** means to _____.
    a. tell people a fib and hope they will not know it
    b. make players think you are going to shoot when you do not plan to shoot it
    c. make players think you will toss a ball one way, and then not toss it that way

Letters and Sounds

You know the word **all.** If you can read **all,** you can read lots of words with the letters **all.** Read these words:

fall   **tall**   **wall**   **mall**

Do you know the word **salt**? It has the same vowel sound as **all.** Read these words:

halt   **Walt**

Do you know the word **walk**? It has the same vowel sound as **all.** But in **walk,** the letter **l** has no sound. It is silent. Read these words.

talk   **stalk**

> **TIP:**   When **a** is followed by **l,** the **a** has the vowel sound in **all.**
>
> If **al** comes before **k,** the **l** is silent.

◆ **Directions:** Write each word again. Circle **al** or **all.**

1. malt _____   5. malted _____

2. call _____   6. caller _____

3. stall _____   7. stalling _____

4. walk _____   8. walked _____

◆ **Directions:** Write each word below where it belongs in the chart.

wall   park   pack   stand
malt   arms   stalk   talk

has the vowel sound in *am*	has the vowel sound in *are*	has the vowel sound in *all*
9. _____ 10. _____	11. _____ 12. _____	13. _____ 14. _____ 15. _____ 16. _____

Story Words

Word Bank

Write each of these story words in the Word Bank at the back of this book.

◆ **Directions:** Read each word to yourself. Then say the word out loud. Write the word on the line. Check the box after each step.

17. away (a | way)   Read ❑ Say ❑ Write ❑ _____

18. point   Read ❑ Say ❑ Write ❑ _____

19. high   Read ❑ Say ❑ Write ❑ _____

20. athlete (ath | lete)   Read ❑ Say ❑ Write ❑ _____

21. believe (be | lieve)   Read ❑ Say ❑ Write ❑ _____

22. coach   Read ❑ Say ❑ Write ❑ _____

More Word Work

◆ **Directions:** Add **ed, ing,** or **er** to each word below.

Example: call + ed = called

23. high + er   = _____

24. walk + ing   = _____

25. halt + ed   = _____

26. talk + ed   = _____

27. believe + er   = _____

28. point + ing   = _____

◆ 29. You had to drop **e** before adding the ending in one word you wrote. Which word was it? _____

◆ **Directions:** Each word below is made of a longer word you know plus an ending. Write each word and the ending that was added to it.

Example: pocketed = pocket + ed

30. remembering = _____ + _____

31. interviewer = _____ + _____

32. fashioned = _____ + _____

33. believing = _____ + _____

Muggsy Bogues steals the ball.

Spud Webb takes the shot.

STAND SMALL, PLAY TALL

Muggsy Bogues, Big on the Court. Tyrone "Muggsy" Bogues is 5'3" tall. Most basketball players in the NBA are way over six feet tall. Some are over seven feet. The basket, at 10 feet high, is almost two times higher than Muggsy is. All this does not stop him from being a great basketball player.

Tyrone, as he was called then, started playing basketball for real in high school. His friend Dwayne Woods was the star of the team and only 5'5" tall. Tyrone was a pest to the other team from the start. He would buzz around the legs of larger players. He would not go away. He played with speed, and he stuck to them to keep them from making an easy shot or pass. One day Dwayne said to Tyrone, "You are out on the court mugging people." This is how he got the name "Muggsy." It **stuck to him** the way he stuck to the game.

Like other short players, Muggsy Bogues puts up with many jokes and **put-downs** about his size. He lets all that kind of talk go by. He just pushes to get better at what he does. Muggsy has blazing speed and fast hands. He can steal the ball away in a flash. He can take the ball down the court like a **walk in the park.** Another of Muggsy's skills is being a great team player. With his nifty passes he helps the other players score more points. He also knows where they need to be, and he helps get them in place. That way, they are set up better for scoring points.

Muggsy Bogues is one of the NBA's all-time leaders in stealing the ball. He is also a leader in getting the ball to another player who scores. His first year in the NBA was 1987. His first coach did not believe in him and did not let him play that much. The next coach put him in as a starter, and away went Muggsy to fame as an NBA player.

Spud Webb: Slam Dunk Champ. Spud Webb is 5'7" tall, only inches taller than Muggsy Bogues. He was one of the smallest basketball players in the NBA in his time. But Spud could leap far into the air, and do it with style. One of his jumps was said to be 44 inches high from a standing start! He was a very fast runner, too. He was able to keep the ball away from others while dribbling it. He made many great passes to let others score. He was a great shooter from the stripe. One year he shot 242 free shots and made 226! He also racked up a lot of points on three-point shots. In 1991–92, playing for Sacramento, he shot 199 long ones and canned 73 of them!

Spud Webb's best skill may be slam dunking the ball. This skill comes from his "big air" jumps. As a kid, at only 4'11", he dunked! In 1986, Spud Webb won the NBA slam dunk contest. That day he walked off with the most points for slam dunks, and he was by far the shortest one out there!

Skill over Size

Small athletes all say one thing to any one who wants to do sports: Go for it! Great athletes like Muggsy Bogues and Spud Webb prove that being smaller in size does not matter in sports. The following points matter more than size:

▲ Know your game and be the best you can be at it.

▲ Take the kinds of gifts you were born with, and work hard to make them into great skills!

▲ Know how to work well with others, not just score points.

▲ Be a leader. Use what you know to help others be better players.

▲ Know you are good and believe it!

▲ Give your all for the team. Give your all to win.

▲ Know and believe you CAN do it.

You Be the Judge

Small athletes like Muggsy Bogues have proved that size may not matter when it comes to playing sports. But there are some jobs where size does matter.

1. Think of some jobs where it is better to be big. Write them on the lines below.

   _____

   _____

2. Think of some jobs where it is better to be smaller in size.

   _____

   _____

Think About the Story

Use Story Words

Directions: Look at your list of story words on page 111. Write a story word on each line.

3. This man or woman tells a team how to play. _____

4. Getting the ball in the basket gets you two of these.

   _____

5. This means "up in the air." _____

6. This means "to think something is so." _____

7. One who can play sports is called this. _____

8. This means "in a place other than this one." _____

What Are the Facts?

Directions: Put a **T** by the sentences that say true things from the story. Put an **F** by the sentences that do not.

9. _____ Muggsy Bogues's real name is Spike.

10. _____ Muggsy Bogues's first year in the NBA was 1987.

11. _____ Muggsy Bogues is a great team player.

12. _____ Spud Webb is good at slam dunks.

13. _____ Spud Webb won a slam dunk contest in 1995.

14. _____ Most NBA players are more than seven feet tall.

Write Sentences About the Story

◆ **Directions:** Use words from the story to answer these questions.

15. How did Tyrone Bogues get the name "Muggsy"?

_____

_____

16. In what ways is Muggsy a great team player?

_____

_____

17. How is Spud Webb like Muggsy Bogues?

_____

_____

18. How is he different as a player?

_____

_____

Words and Meanings

◆ **Directions:** Think about how the **bold** words are used in the story. Then circle the words that show the meaning of each word or phrase.

19. In this story, a **walk in the park** is _____.
    a. a nice walk under the trees
    b. a very easy task
    c. a job that is hard to do

20. Tyrone's new name Muggsy **stuck to him.** This means _____.
    a. he could not peel it off
    b. he does not feel good about his size
    c. people kept calling him that

21. To **put down** someone means to _____.
    a. say bad things about him or her
    b. put him or her back down on the ground
    c. tell fibs about him or her

Chapter 2: Summary of Skills and Strategies

Let's look back at what you learned in Chapter 2.

Letters and Sounds

◆ You learned that . . .

  ▸ sometimes two letters, like **kn** and **wr,** can stand for just one sound.

  ▸ when a vowel is followed by **r,** the vowel stands for a sound that is not long or short.

  ▸ a vowel followed by **l** has a sound that is not long or short.

Stories and Skills

◆ You learned about . . .

  ▸ characters who faced problems and found solutions.

  ▸ strange tales from the desert.

  ▸ a real-life woman who had a great idea for a small business.

  ▸ basketball players who "stand small, but play tall."

◆ You learned . . .

  ▸ how to use what you know to help you understand what you read.

  ▸ how to look ahead, or predict, what might happen in a story.

Words and Meanings

◆ You learned . . .

  ▸ a lot of new words.

  ▸ how to add **ly** to words.

  ▸ how to add **'s** to show that something belongs to someone.

  ▸ how to add **er** to a word to make it mean "one who."

The chapter review will give you a chance to show what you have learned.

Part A

Summing It Up: Letters and Sounds

> ▶ The letters **kn** can come at the beginning of a word. They stand for the **n** sound in **not.**
> ▶ The letters **wr** can come at the beginning of a word. They stand for the **r** sound in **ran.**

◆ **Directions:** Write each word below in the list where it belongs.

know	wren	knot
wreck	knife	knee
write	wrap	

Begins like *not*	Begins like *ran*
1. _____	5. _____
2. _____	6. _____
3. _____	7. _____
4. _____	8. _____

> ▶ The letters **ge** can come at the end of a word. They stand for the **j** sound in **age.**
> ▶ The letters **dge** can come at the end of a word. They stand for the **j** sound in **lodge.**

◆ **Directions:** Draw a line under each word that has the **j** sound. Then circle the letter or letters that stand for that sound

9. leg	**12.** hug	**15.** rage	**18.** fig
10. huge	**13.** rag	**16.** judge	
11. ledge	**14.** ridge	**17.** smudge	

▸ The letters **th, sh, ch,** and **wh** come at the beginning of some words. They stand for one sound.

▸ The letters **th, sh, ch, wh,** and **tch** come at the end of some words. They stand for one sound.

Directions: Write each word where it belongs in the chart.

sheep	chick	thick	such
wheel	ship	math	fish
chat	rich	sash	thin
which	pitch	match	bath

Begins like . . . *thing*	*show*	*chin*	*what*
19. _____ _____	20. _____ _____	21. _____ _____	22. _____ _____

Ends like . . . *path*	*dish*	*much*	*itch*
23. _____ _____	24. _____ _____	25. _____ _____ _____	26. _____ _____

▸ When **a** is followed by **l,** the **a** has the vowel sound in **all.**

▸ If **al** comes before **k,** the **l** is silent.

Directions: Write each word where it belongs in the chart.

small	dark	talk	smack
halt	pack	mark	sharp

vowel sound in *am*	vowel sound in *are*	vowel sound in *all*
27. _____	29. _____	32. _____
28. _____	30. _____	33. _____
	31. _____	34. _____

▸ When a vowel is followed by **r,** the vowel stands for a sound that is not long or short.

▸ The letters **or** and **ore** stand for the vowel plus **r** sound in **for** and **more.**

▸ The letters **er** and **ir** stand for the vowel plus **r** sound in **her** and **fir.**

▸ The letters **ar** stand for the vowel plus **r** sound in **far.**

◆ **Directions:** Write each word where it belongs in the chart.

whir	stern	bore	stir
tar	torn	fern	cards
core	farm	smart	shore

vowel plus *r* sound in *for*	vowel plus *r* sound in *far*	vowel plus *r* sound in *her* and *fir*
35. _____	39. _____	43. _____
36. _____	40. _____	44. _____
37. _____	41. _____	45. _____
38. _____	42. _____	46. _____

▸ The letters **nk** stand for one sound—the sound you hear at the end of **pink.**

▸ The letters **ng** have one sound—the sound you hear at the end of **sing.**

◆ **Directions:** Find four sets of words that rhyme. Write them on the lines.

think	spent	sung	ink
hung	land	rent	sand

47. _____   _____

48. _____   _____

49. _____   _____

50. _____   _____

Part B

Summing It Up: More Word Work

> ▸ You can use **'s** to show that a thing belongs to a person, place, or thing.

Directions: Write each sentence again. Use **'s** to show that something belongs to a person, place, or thing.

Example: The dog the man has is cute.
    The man's dog is cute.

1. The car Jesse has needs fixing.

   _____

2. The cake Jamal made came out flat.

   _____

3. The gold in that mine has all been taken.

   _____

> ▸ When the letters **th, sh, ch,** or **tch** come together in a word, they stay together when you split the word into syllables.
>
> ▸ When you split a word with the vowel plus **r** sound into syllables, the vowel and the **r** always stay together.

Directions: Write each word again. Draw a line to split the word into syllables.

Example: pitching   pitch | ing

4. richer   _____

5. ditching   _____

6. batches   _____

7. numbering   _____

8. stirring   _____

9. boring   _____

▶ The ending **er** can mean "one who." You can add **er** to many words to make them tell about someone who does something.

Directions: Add **er** to each word. Write the word in the sentence.

Examples: write → My mom is a writer.

swim → That swimmer is fast!

10. sell → I am the _____ of the bike.

11. win → Who is the _____ of the race?

12. drive → Dan is a fine _____.

Part C

Story Words

Directions: On the lines below, write the word from the list that matches each clue.

large	high	small	alien
also	three	athlete	girl
play	desert	friend	shoot

1. a hot, dry place _____

2. one who is good at sports _____

3. not a boy _____

4. a being from space _____

5. a good pal _____

6. up, up, up _____

7. big in size _____

8. means "and" _____

9. try to get a ball into a basket _____

10. take part in a game _____

11. one, two, _____ _____

12. means "little" _____

Directions: On the lines below, write a word from the list to finish each sentence.

style	hood	surprise
too	ghost	gold
area	believe	under
coach		

13. Jacob Walzer killed for _____.

14. I turned as white as a _____.

15. I got a big _____ when I saw a snake in my car.

16. Look _____ the bed for your socks.

17. My _____ helps me with my game.

18. Lift up the _____ of the car.

19. I like grapes. Chad likes them, _____.

20. This _____ is rocky and dry.

21. A hat gives you some _____.

22. I _____ I am the best one for the job.

Directions: Read each word. On the lines below, write a number to tell how many syllables the word has.

23. basketball _____   29. any _____

24. fashion _____   30. around _____

25. rubber _____   31. does _____

26. another _____   32. barefoot _____

27. court _____   33. follow _____

28. away _____   34. prove _____

◆ **Directions:** On the lines below, write the word from the list that matches each clue.

boy	point	here	because
want	even	kind	move
show	put		

35. to set something down _____

36. means "to not be still" _____

37. means "in this place" _____

38. means "wish for something" _____

39. what a score of 10 to 10 is _____

40. what you get when you score _____

41. put something down for people to see _____

42. a word that tells why _____

43. not a girl _____

44. very, very nice to others _____

Who Did This?

◆ **Directions:** This list has the names of the real people who were in the stories in Chapter 2. Write a name to answer each question.

the Apaches	Muggsy Bogues	Spud Webb
Ramon Peralta	Lamar Odom	Jacob Walzer
Ave Green	the U.S. Air Force	

45. Who was the winner of a slam dunk contest? _____

46. Who killed Ramon Peralta? _____

47. Who started a fashion trend? _____

48. Who "mugs people" on the court? _____

49. Who killed the Peraltas and hid their mine? _____

50. Who sports a rubber band on his wrist? _____

51. Who says Area 51 is a place for testing planes? _____

52. Who let an old man know where a gold mine was? _____

What Kind of Story?

◆ **Directions:** Write **nonfiction** next to the stories that tell about real people or places. Write **fiction** next to the stories that were made up.

53. "The Girl in the Desert" _____

54. "Tales from the Desert" _____

55. "Stretching the Limits" _____

56. "The Surprise Star" _____

57. "Stand Small, Play Tall" _____

Part D

Think About the Stories

Who Did That?

◆ **Directions:** Write the name of a story character to answer each question.

Franky	Sly	Jamal
Riff	Ann	Tyrell

1. Who proved something on a basketball court?_____

2. Who had a car that broke down? _____

3. Who surprised people by fixing a car? _____

4. Who called a short kid "Flea-Boy"? _____

5. Who went on a trip in another kid's car?
_____ and _____

Where Did It Happen?

◆ **Directions:** Write each place name by the story it goes with.

a diner	The Lost Dutchman Mine
city basketball courts	Area 51
Superstition Mountains	St. Paul
Old Rage Ridge	L.A.

6. "The Girl in the Desert" _____

7. "Tales of the Desert" _____

8. "The Surprise Star" _____

9. "Stretching the Limits" _____

CHAPTER 3

Letters and Sounds

> **TIPS:** ▶ Sometimes three consonants come together at the beginning of a word.
>
> ▶ In the blends **scr, str,** and **spr,** each letter stands for one sound. You can hear three sounds at the beginning of **scrap, strip,** and **spring**.
>
> ▶ The letters **squ** stand for this sound: **skw. Squ** stands for the sound at the beginning of the word **squirrel**.
>
> ▶ The letters in **shr** and **thr** stand for two sounds. You can hear two sounds at the beginning of **shrink** and **threw**.

◆ **Directions:** Read each word. Circle the three letters at the beginning of each word.

1. three	**4.** string	**7.** sprint
2. stretch	**5.** shred	**8.** through
3. sprig	**6.** squid	**9.** squint

◆ **Directions:** Write each word next to the sentence that tells about it.

10. This means "run fast for a short while." _____

11. This is a number. _____

12. This lives in the sea and squirts ink. _____

13. This is long and thin and used for wrapping. _____

14. This is a way of looking at things. _____

15. This word tells what you can do to rubber. _____

16. This is a thing with a leaf or two. _____

17. This means "rip into little bits." _____

18. This means "into and beyond." _____

◆ **Directions:** Write the letters on the lines. See how many words you can make.

irt	unk	ift	ap	ink	eeze	ill	ipt

19. thr _____	**21.** shr _____	**23.** squ _____	**25.** scr _____
20. thr _____	**22.** shr _____	**24.** squ _____	**26.** scr _____

Story Words

Directions: Read each word to yourself. Then say the word out loud. Write the word on the line. Check the box after each step.

27. animal (an | i | mal) Read ❑ Say ❑ Write ❑ _____

28. house Read ❑ Say ❑ Write ❑ _____

29. mother (moth | er) Read ❑ Say ❑ Write ❑ _____

30. counselor (coun | sel | or) Read ❑ Say ❑ Write ❑ _____

31. food Read ❑ Say ❑ Write ❑ _____

32. burger (bur | ger) Read ❑ Say ❑ Write ❑ _____

More Word Work

Let's sum up what you know about words and endings.

- You can add **s** or **es** to many words.
- You can add **ed** or **ing** to many words.
- You can add **ly** to some words. **Ly** means "in a way that is."
- You can add **'s** to show that something belongs to a person, place, or thing.
- You can add **er** to some words. **Er** can mean "one who."
- Sometimes you have to drop **e** or double the last consonant when you add an ending.

Directions: Add an ending to each word. Write the new word on the line.

Examples: neat + ly = neatly
drum + ing = drumming
blame + ed = blamed

33. friend + ly = _____

34. prove + ed = _____

35. coach + ing = _____

36. ghost + ly = _____

37. help + er = _____

38. live + ing = _____

39. run + er = _____

Use What You Know

In this story, a city kid named Kevin takes a job as a counselor-in-training at a camp for little kids. Why might being at a camp be hard for a city kid? Write what you think.

_____

_____

_____

Then read to find out what camp is like for Kevin.

CAMP COUNSELOR, PART 1

"So you know the rules, Kevin? Say them back to me." Mike Strong, the boss at Camp Spring Hill, looked right at Kevin. About then, Kevin Walker was wishing he was back in his mother's house in the city. "At least her food is good," Kevin was thinking. This was Kevin's first summer job. He was a counselor-in-training. His job was to help the lead counselors with the campers at Camp Spring Hill. If he did well this year, he could be a lead counselor next year. **"Big deal,"** Kevin was thinking.

Kevin started to spell out the long list of rules. "Yes, I know the rules, Mike," Kevin said. "No food in the houses. I mean, the cabins. No animals in the cabins. Keep the house clean. I mean, the cabin. Make the campers keep their beds, I mean, **bunks,** neat. Keep the campers from playing on the top bunks. Get them to write at least a one-page letter to their mothers, or to home. No shooting peas or other food in the **mess hall.**"

Kevin was thinking that this job was like being a mother! Only where was the nice home? Where was the good food? He was having a hard time. He did not like being away from the city. He missed the city sounds. He missed TV. He was thinking, "Look at this place. It is only tree bark, pine cones, rocks, and stones. After dark, there are screeching animals. What if a large animal jumps out at me while I am hiking? What if I fall, and it squeezes my guts out? What if it bites off my hand or leg? What then?"

And he hated the camp food. "I wish I could call that stuff food. Why does it have to be so bad? It is one kind of mush in the morning, another kind of mush for lunch, and even more mush for dinner." What he would give for some good fast food, just one time! His taste buds woke up when he dreamed of a hot burger and a frothy milk shake.

Just then, Mike Strong woke Kevin up from his day-dreaming. "Your kids are here, Kevin," he said. "Go and take them up to the cabin. Tell them the camp rules. Show them where things are. Then you can let them have some free time. The dinner bell, as you know, rings at 6:00 sharp."

What do you think will happen next? Will Kevin ever like the camp? Will he get along with the campers? Write what you think on the lines below. Then keep reading to find out what happens.

_____

_____

Kevin looked at the five little boys. They were standing under the tall pine trees. "Okay, let's have a race. First one to find cabin number five gets first pick of bunks." The boys raced up the walk to find the cabin. "Looks like a bunch of athletes, all right," Kevin was thinking. "These boys may make a good basketball team. In a bit, I will take them up to the courts and see if they can play. Let them prove to me how well they can shoot."

It turned out that the first week went OK. The campers wrote letters to their mothers. Only one boy fell out of a top bunk. The boys were good at basketball and at scrubbing dishes. Then it was the day for the campout. The kids would hike away from the main camp. They would set up a little camp and sleep out under the stars. As it turned out, the lead cabin counselor was sick that day. It was up to Kevin to lead the outing.

He and his campers set out after lunch. Kevin kept the boys moving north through the trees. He had a plan, and it was all about getting some good food. There was a fast food burger place about a mile north of the cabins. His plan was to get close to the burger place. Then he could sneak out of the camp. He could get some real food! He planned to treat all the boys to burgers and shakes.

Kevin and the boys stopped at a high point. They put out their sleeping bags and set up their tent. Then he let the boys in on his plan. The boys were to stick close to the camp while he snuck out to get the burgers. He said, "I will be back before you know it." ▶

You Be the Judge

◆ 1. Do you think Kevin's plan to get some fast food is a good one? Why or why not? Write what you think on the lines below.

_____

_____

_____

Think About the Story

Use Story Words

◆ **Directions:** Look at your list of story words on page 127. Write a story word on each line.

2. This is another word for "mom."   _____

3. People live in this.   _____

4. This is made up of meat and a bun.   _____

5. This tells what a dog and a cat are.   _____

6. This comes in many forms and you can eat all of them.   _____

7. This is someone who is in charge of campers.   _____

When Did It Happen?

◆ 8. Write a number from 1 to 6 in front of each event to show when it happened.

_____ Kevin meets his five campers for the first time.

_____ The lead camp counselor gets sick.

_____ Kevin and his campers pitch a tent.

_____ Kevin leads his boys out of camp.

_____ Kevin goes off looking for burgers.

_____ Mike Strong asks Kevin to say the rules back to him.

Write Sentences About the Story

9. How does Kevin feel about being at camp? Use words from the list to write one or two sentences about Kevin.

mother	food	camp
rules	trees	misses

_____

_____

Words and Meanings

Directions: Think about how the **bold** words are used in the story. Then circle the words that show the meaning of each word or phrase.

10. When Kevin thinks, **"Big deal,"** he means _____.
 a. "What a great job!"
 b. "What is so great about that?"
 c. "I can hardly wait!"

11. In this story, a **mess hall** is _____.
 a. a huge dining hall
 b. a place where campers sleep
 c. a big messy tent

12. In this story, **bunks** are _____.
 a. animals that come around in the dark
 b. bumps on a log
 c. beds where campers sleep

What Are the Facts?

Directions: Write **T** by the sentences that tell about Camp Spring Hill. Write **F** by the sentences that do not.

13. _____ It is in a city.

14. _____ Animals live by the camp.

15. _____ It is a camp just for girls.

16. _____ Teens can get trained as counselors.

Look Ahead

17. What do you think will happen when the boys camp out? Write what you think on the lines below. Then read on to find out.

_____

_____

Letters and Sounds

◆ **Directions:** These words have the long **a** sound. Circle the vowel or vowels in each word.

1. made   2. main   3. grade   4. pain

> **TIP:** The **a**-consonant-**e** pattern stands for the long **a** sound. The letters **ai** stand for the long **a** sound.

◆ **Directions:** Read these words. Circle each one that has the long **a** sound.

5. same   8. glade   11. stands   14. fail

6. pail   9. snaps   12. fade   15. strands

7. fast   10. grain   13. stain   16. male

◆ **Directions:** Write the words you circled under the word that has the same pattern of letters for long **a**.

main	grade
17. _____	21. _____
18. _____	22. _____
19. _____	23. _____
20. _____	24. _____

◆ **Directions:** Write the letters on the lines. See how many words you can make.

g	st	sn	t	m	p	qu	n	tr

25. _____ ail   30. _____ ain

26. _____ ail   31. _____ ain

27. _____ ail   32. _____ ain

28. _____ ail   33. _____ ain

29. _____ ail   34. _____ ain

Story Words

Directions: Read each word to yourself. Then say the word out loud. Write the word on the line. Check the box after each step.

35. answer (an | swer) Read ❏ Say ❏ Write ❏ _____

36. found Read ❏ Say ❏ Write ❏ _____

37. light Read ❏ Say ❏ Write ❏ _____

38. spray Read ❏ Say ❏ Write ❏ _____

39. question (ques | tion) Read ❏ Say ❏ Write ❏ _____

Word Bank

Write each of these story words in the Word Bank at the back of this book.

More Word Work

You know that adding **e** to a word like **dim** or **man** gives the word a long vowel sound. You know that words like **dime** and **mane** have the consonant-vowel-consonant-**e** pattern, or CVC**e**.

Two vowels next to each other can also have a long vowel sound. **Mean, need,** and **main** are examples. These words have the consonant-vowel-vowel-consonant pattern, or CVVC.

Directions: Read each word. Circle the vowels in the word.

40. peach	43. train	46. pale	49. game
41. dime	44. seed	47. fail	50. tune
42. home	45. main	48. team	51. brain

Directions: Write each word in the chart where it belongs.

CVC*e* pattern	CVVC pattern
52. _____	57. _____
53. _____	58. _____
54. _____	59. _____
55. _____	60. _____
56. _____	61. _____
	62. _____
	63. _____

> **TIP:** When two vowels go walking, the first one usually does the talking.

CAMP COUNSELOR, PART 2

"Boy, these kids will like me a lot," Kevin was thinking as he made his way through the trees. "What other counselor would do this for his campers?" He just hoped no animals would show up to wreck the fun.

Kevin did not have a hard time finding the fast food place. He got six milk shakes and six burgers. Kevin then walked back into the camp. He was safe—no other campers or staff got a look at him. Back at the camp, he called the boys over. They all got into the tent. They had a great time downing those burgers and shakes. They were not following the camp rules. They were proving that they could make up some new rules at Camp Spring Hill. And that food tasted so good.

Then Kevin had the boys scrunch up the drink cups and the burger wrappings. They squished all this down into the back corner of the tent. That way, no other campers or counselors would see their food trash.

After dark, Kevin and the boys sat around and talked about how good those burgers and shakes were. Then Kevin started telling ghost tales. He liked giving those kids some thrills and chills. The boys liked him. "What other counselor is as funny as I am?" Kevin was thinking. The campers even seemed to believe his tales. They liked it when he screamed out or played tricks on them.

Then it got late. They all went to sleep. Kevin had a hard time at first. The **shrill** cry of this or that animal out in the dark kept him up. At last, he got to sleep, too.

They must have drifted off for some time. All of a sudden, Kevin woke up. A thing was scratching at the tent. No! A thing was in the tent. An animal! An animal was in the tent! But what animal? It was dark, so Kevin could not see it. But he could smell it. And it did not smell good.

What kind of animal do you think got into the tent? Write what you think on the lines below. Then read on to find out what happened next.

_____

_____

Kevin grabbed for his flash light and turned it on. He found out the answer to his question. It was a skunk! No, look here! It was a mother skunk and two small skunks. The black and white animals were all the way in the back corner of the tent. Kevin could not help but let out a kind of scratchy screech. The other boys woke right up. In a flash, Kevin remembered the fast food wrappers. The skunks were after the food wrappers!

The mother skunk turned and gave the boys one look. Then it raised its tail up high in the air. It pointed its back side at the boys. Then it **let go,** shooting a blast of skunk spray all over the place. The smell was way strong. The small skunks raised their tails up high and let go, too. Then all the skunks ran out of the tent.

The boys **bailed out** of the tent in pain, screaming for air. It was too late. They and all their sleeping bags, plus the tent, were blasted by the spray. What a rotten, smelly mess!

The sounds from Kevin's camp reached the main camp. When Mike Strong got out to the spot, all five boys were wailing and crying. Their things had skunk stains all over them. They could not get away from the smell. Kevin answered each one of Mike Strong's many questions. Kevin said he had just wanted to have some fun. He had not been thinking things through. He had only wanted the campers to like him.

The next day, Kevin spent a lot of time in the dog house. At first, the other counselors wanted to send him home. To Kevin's surprise, he did not want to go home. In the end, the counselors let Kevin go back to his kids. "You are still a counselor-in-training," Mike said. "And I believe you can do this job. But you must not slip up one more time."

Kevin could only think, "Now I know why the camp rules say, 'No food in the cabins!'"

You Be the Judge

1. Were the lead counselors right to let Kevin keep his job at Camp Spring Hill? Why or why not? Write what you think on the lines below.

_____

_____

_____

2. What would you have done if you were Mike Strong?

_____

_____

Think About the Story

Use Story Words

Directions: Look at your list of story words on page 133. Write a story word on each line.

3. You see this when the sun comes up. _____

4. A skunk does this when it is mad. _____

5. This is what you ask. _____

6. This is what you give when someone asks you something. _____

7. This is a form of **find**. _____

Why Did It Happen?

Directions: Draw a line from each event to the reason it happened.

What Happened	Why
8. Skunks went into the tent.	○ Three skunks sprayed the tent.
9. The boys ran outside screaming.	○ Kevin wanted the campers to like him.
10. Kevin broke the camp rules.	○ Animals were making sounds.
11. Kevin had a hard time sleeping.	○ Fast food wrappers were scrunched up in the tent.

Words and Meanings

Directions: Think about how the **bold** words are used in the story. Then circle the words that show the meaning of each word or phrase.

12. A **shrill** cry is _____.
    a. soft and sweet
    b. very far away
    c. high and sharp

13. When the boys **bailed out** of the tent, they _____.
    a. ran out fast
    b. filed out in a line
    c. asked Kevin to pick them up

14. The little skunks **let go,** too. This means they _____.
    a. put the food wrappers down
    b. sprayed just like their mother
    c. let go of Kevin's leg

The Big Idea

15. Which sentence best sums up the story? Circle that sentence.
    a. A boy finds a way to get burgers and shakes, even at camp.
    b. A counselor-in-training finds out why rules are needed.
    c. Three skunks raid a tent and spray some people.

Write Sentences About the Story

Directions: Use words from the story to answer these questions.

16. What did Kevin see in the tent when he turned on the light?

_____

_____

17. Was Kevin glad to see the animals? Why or why not?

_____

_____

18. Why did Mike Strong ask Kevin a lot of questions?

_____

_____

Letters and Sounds

Directions: Read these words. Circle the words that have the long **i** sound.

1. dim	**4.** slip	**7.** my	**9.** time
2. pine	**5.** light	**8.** grip	**10.** by
3. high	**6.** mine		

> **TIP:** Many patterns of letters can stand for the long **i** sound. The letters **igh** and the letter **y** can stand for the long **i** sound.

Directions: Read these words. Circle the letter or letters that stand for long **i** in each word.

11. high	**12.** my	**13.** light	**14.** by

Directions: Write each word above under the word that has the same pattern of letters for long **i**.

try	tight
15. _____	**17.** _____
16. _____	**18.** _____

Directions: Write the letters on the lines. See how many words you can make.

f	fl	br	fr	m	cr	pl	tr	t	r

19. _____ ight	**24.** _____ y
20. _____ ight	**25.** _____ y
21. _____ ight	**26.** _____ y
22. _____ ight	**27.** _____ y
23. _____ ight	**28.** _____ y

Story Words

Directions: Read each word to yourself. Then say the word out loud. Write the word on the line. Check the box after each step.

29. study   Read ❑ Say ❑ Write ❑   _____

30. learn   Read ❑ Say ❑ Write ❑   _____

31. million (mil | lion)   Read ❑ Say ❑ Write ❑   _____

32. serve   Read ❑ Say ❑ Write ❑   _____

33. service (ser | vice)   Read ❑ Say ❑ Write ❑   _____

More Word Work

You know that you can add the endings **es** and **ed** to many words. What happens when you add these endings to a word that ends in **y**? Here's what happens:

$$\textbf{try + es = tries} \qquad \textbf{try + ed = tried}$$

34. What letter in **try** was changed when the endings were added? _____

35. What letter took the place of **y**? _____

> **TIP:** When you add **es** or **ed** to a word that ends in **y**, change the **y** to **i**. Then add the ending.

Directions: Add **es** to each word. Write the new word on the line. Change **y** to **i**.

Example: cry + ed = cried

36. spy + es = _____   38. try + ed = _____

37. fly + es = _____   39. guppy + es = _____

> **TIP:** When you add **ing** to a word that ends in **y**, do not drop the **y**. Just add the ending.

Example: fry + ing = frying

Directions: Add **es, ed,** or **ing** to each word below.

40. spy + ed = _____   42. try + ing = _____

41. fly + ing = _____   43. puppy + es = _____

Use What You Know

Do you have friends who have jobs? What kinds of jobs do they have? What other kinds of jobs do teens do? Write what you think on the lines below. Then read on to find out about jobs for teens.

_____

_____

_____

_____

SUMMER JOBS FOR TEENS

So June is here and school is out. Are you thinking about getting a job? Here are some questions for you to answer about the kind of work you might like to do:

▲ Do you want to work days or nights?

▲ Do you like to be **out in the open air,** such as at a camp or park?

▲ Are you willing to go out of the area to work?

▲ What have you learned to do? What training have you had? What did you study in school?

▲ Do you like to work with people? Do you want to be the boss?

◆ Facts about summer jobs

Some teens work while they are still in school. Even more teens have summer jobs. Here are some things you might like to know about summer jobs for teens. These facts tell about U.S. teens 15 to 17 years of age.

▲ About 4 million teens, or one out of three, work at a summer job.

▲ Most make **wages** of $5.38 to $5.65. Some teens are paid a higher wage, and some are paid less.

▲ Teens work in many kinds of jobs. About 2 million of those who have jobs work in some kind of sales job, such as in a store. About 1.3 million kids have jobs having to do with service. Service means any kind of job that has to do with helping people. A camp counselor and a food server have service jobs.

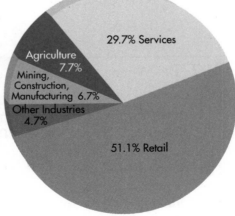

Employed persons 15 to 17 years of age by industry, summer months

◆ Be the boss

Some teens run the show when it comes to work. Here are some jobs you might do:

- ▲ **Pet sitting.** Many people need their dogs, cats, or other animals fed, walked, brushed, or cleaned up after.
- ▲ **Yard work.** Many people need help in their yards. This means cutting grass, raking leaves, getting rid of weeds, planting things, and trimming trees or shrubs.
- ▲ **Cleaning houses or other places.**
- ▲ **Painting houses, barns, stores, or other places.**
- ▲ **Looking after kids.**
- ▲ **Making or baking food.**
- ▲ **Helping others with their school work.** What are your strong points? If you are an athlete, you might train others.

◆ More jobs for teens

Still waiting for the light to go on about what kind of job to try for? Think about where you have seen teens at work. Teens may work in stores at the mall, at fast food places, or in other small stores close to their homes. Some teens work for their mothers or dads, or for other people they know. Here is a list of places that may hire teens for summer jobs:

- ▲ **Golf, tennis, or swim clubs.** Kids might help keep things clean. Or they might help teach smaller kids, if they have the skills.
- ▲ **Summer camps or city parks.** Some kids work as counselors or counselors-in-training. Others cut grass and trim shrubs.
- ▲ **Fast food places.** Do you have friends who flip burgers or serve food? This could be a good job for you.
- ▲ **Theme parks.** Selling things, helping with food, and learning to greet people are some of the jobs at theme parks.
- ▲ **Stores at a mall.** Many teens work as baggers or **stockers** who take goods out of boxes and put them out for sale.

These are not the only kinds of jobs for teens. Think about what kind of job you might like. What jobs are you thinking about right now? Write about them on the lines below.

_____

_____

_____

_____

_____

What Do You Think?

◆ 1. What jobs sound like fun to you? What jobs do not sound like fun? Write what you think on the lines below.

_____

_____

_____

Think About the Story

Use Story Words

◆ **Directions:** Look at your list of story words on page 139. Write a story word on each line.

2. Sometimes you must do this to learn
   something.   _____

3. This means "to do for others."   _____

4. This is a very big number!   _____

5. You do this when you get new skills.   _____

6. This kind of job has to do with
   helping people.   _____

Write Sentences About the Story

◆ **Directions:** Use words from the story to answer these questions.

7. About how many teens work at summer jobs?

_____

_____

8. What is a service job?

_____

9. Did more teens work in sales jobs or in service jobs?

_____

10. What are some ways teen workers can "be the boss"?

_____

_____

_____

_____

Your Turn

◆ What if you could have any job you wanted? What would it be? Write what you think on the lines below.

_____

_____

◆ Say you started a small business. Use this space to make up an ad. In the ad, tell people what you can do for them.

My Name: _____

What I Do: _____

_____

_____

_____

Why You Should Call Me: _____

_____

_____

_____

Words and Meanings

◆ **Directions:** Think about how the **bold** words are used in the story. Then circle the words that show the meaning of each word or phrase.

11. A **wage** is _____.
    a. the wagging of a dog's tail
    b. another word for **age**
    c. how much someone makes at a job

12. A **stocker** is a worker who _____.
    a. sells stocks and bonds
    b. puts stuff on store shelves
    c. plays for a sports team

13. Which place is **out in the open air**? _____.
    a. a mall
    b. a park
    c. a fast food place

Letters and Sounds

These words have the long **o** sound:

slope   boat   hole   float

> **TIP:** ▸ The letter pattern **o**-consonant-**e** stands for the long **o** sound.
>
> ▸ The letters **oa** stand for the long **o** sound.

◆ **Directions:** Read these words. Circle the words that have the long **o** sound.

1. hopped	4. moat	7. bloat	10. shot
2. hope	5. choke	8. chopped	11. spoke
3. wrote	6. drop	9. groaned	12. foam

◆ **Directions:** Write each word you circled under the word that has the same pattern of letters for long **o**.

slope	float
13. _____	17. _____
14. _____	18. _____
15. _____	19. _____
16. _____	20. _____

◆ **Directions:** Write the letters on the lines. See how many words you can make.

fl	t	b	z	c	st	m	bl

21. _____ oat   25. _____ one

22. _____ oat   26. _____ one

23. _____ oat   27. _____ one

24. _____ oat   28. _____ one

Story Words

◆ **Directions:** Read each word to yourself. Then say the word out loud. Write the word on the line. Check the box after each step.

29. picture (pic | ture)   Read ❑ Say ❑ Write ❑   _____

30. again (a | gain)   Read ❑ Say ❑ Write ❑   _____

31. change   Read ❑ Say ❑ Write ❑   _____

32. letter (let | ter)   Read ❑ Say ❑ Write ❑   _____

33. thought   Read ❑ Say ❑ Write ❑   _____

34. idea (i | de | a)   Read ❑ Say ❑ Write ❑   _____

Word Bank

Write each of these story words in the Word Bank at the back of this book.

More Word Work

> **TIP:** Some words are made up of two smaller words that have been put together. These are called **compound** words. **Someone** and **something** are compound words.

◆ **Directions:** Read each word. Look for two smaller words that make it up. Write the two smaller words on the lines.

Example: someone = some + one

35. anyone   = _____ + _____

36. boathouse = _____ + _____

37. campout   = _____ + _____

38. highway   = _____ + _____

39. homework = _____ + _____

> **TIP:** If a compound word has two syllables, divide the word between the two smaller words that make it up.
> boat | house

◆ **Directions:** Draw a line from each word in column 1 to a word in column 2. Make three compound words. Then write the words.

40. some   ○ boat   43. _____

41. with   ○ where   44. _____

42. sail   ○ out   45. _____

THE LETTERS

Dan spotted the corner of the letter sticking out from his locker. He opened the locker and tore open the note. For three days it had been the same thing, without a change. At the end of lunch, he found a letter in his locker. But who was writing them?

Like the others, this was a one-page note. It had a sketched picture of a boy and girl. It had one question: "Are you going to the party on Friday night?" Again and again, all the notes ended with the code name "Out of Sight." The other notes had said:

"I like you but I am shy. I do not know the road to reach you."

"I am out of sight, but I am also very close by."

"You are **one in a million**. I might tell you who I am someday."

Dan looked around. He felt as if the writer of the letters might be looking at him, even now. Maybe he would see her! Dan thought to himself, "How can I answer the letters if I do not know who the writer is? How can I learn who she is?" Dan studied the note in his hand. Then he had an idea. "I know. These notes are here each day after lunch, at 12:30, without fail. What if I eat lunch faster and make a point of getting here by 12:20 for a change? That is how I will catch the writer of the notes."

The next day, Dan got to his locker at 12:20 sharp. As he came around the corner, he spotted a girl walking away from the area by his locker. It was Jenny, a girl from his French class. He went to his locker. Yes! Again, a note was scrunched through a vent opening. It had a picture of a sailboat on some water, with waves and spray around the boat. The picture also showed a boy and a girl in the boat. This note had two sentences: "I like you. I do not know how to tell you this, but **you float my boat!**" Dan thought, "I bet Jenny is writing these notes to me! It has to be!"

Do you think Jenny is the writer of the notes? Circle your answer.

YES   NO

Why or why not? Write what you think on the lines below.

_____

_____

Then keep reading to find out who is writing the notes to Dan.

The next day, Dan crammed down his lunch and rushed to his locker by 12:15. Again, Jenny was just walking away around a corner. Dan peeked around the corner. He spotted Jenny going up to her friend Skye. Skye was talking to Coach Reed, a counselor and track coach. Coach Reed said good-bye. Then Jenny started talking with Skye. Dan started to walk by them. Catching sight of him, Jenny and Skye stopped talking. They looked off the other way, as if they did not see him. Very strange! Dan just walked by them, without saying anything. He could feel Skye looking at him closely. Inside, Dan felt that "Out of Sight" had to be Jenny. After all, he kept seeing her by his locker!

The next day, Dan had an idea. "If I can just see Jenny's handwriting," he thought, "I can prove that she is the writer of the notes." He walked by her desk. Without making a big deal out of it, he looked at her handwriting. This was strange. It did not match the handwriting on the notes!

Dan felt **stumped**. Then he had another idea. He grabbed a pen from his backpack and jotted a fast note on a blank page. It said, "I like you, too! Talk to me." On the outside of the note he wrote, "To: Out of Sight. From: Dan." The bell rang. He picked up his coat and backpack, and brushed past Jenny. He slipped the note into the pocket of her backpack, with just the corner showing. Then he hung back so he could follow her without being seen. "Now I will be the one who is out of sight," he thought. Jenny met Skye at the food line. The two girls went outside with their burgers. They sat down by some plants to eat. Dan followed them. He tried to keep out of sight. He sat down on the other side of the plants. The girls did not see him, but he could see them through the leaves.

Jenny set down her backpack. She spied the note and opened it. She cried out, "Look, Skye! How thrilling! It's a note from Dan!" She had a big smile on her face. "He says he likes me! This is funny! He thinks that I am 'Out of Sight.' He does not know that you wrote the notes, not me!"

Skye was not smiling. "This does not thrill me at all!" she cried. "I like Dan, but now he is writing to you. This changes things! He likes you, not me!" She looked sad and mad at the same time.

Dan felt shocked. It was Skye who wrote the notes. It was Skye who liked him, not Jenny. He had not pictured this. Now what? ▶

What Do You Think?

◆ 1. Is writing a note and sticking it in a locker a good way to tell someone you like him? Why or why not? What is a better way? Write what you think on the lines below.

_____

_____

_____

Think About the Story

Use Story Words

◆ **Directions:** Look at your list of story words on page 145. Write a story word on each line.

2. You can write a _____ to a friend.

3. To do something one more time is to do it _____.

4. Hang a _____ on a wall.

5. At dusk, day will _____ to night.

6. _____ and _____ mean almost the same thing.

Write Sentences About the Story

◆ **Directions:** Use words from the story to answer each question.

7. Who found a letter in his locker?

_____

8. What code name did the sender use?

_____

_____

9. What was Dan's plan for catching the note writer?

_____

_____

10. What surprised Dan?

_____

_____

Words and Meanings

◆ **Directions:** Think about how the **bold** words are used in the story. Then circle the words that show the meaning of each word or phrase.

11. In the story, **one in a million** means _____.
    a. someone who is like no other
    b. one kid stuck in a crowd of a million kids
    c. one kid with a million bucks

12. The note writer tells Dan, **"You float my boat."** What is she really saying?
    a. "I want to go sailing with you."
    b. "I think you are great."
    c. "Will you float this for me?"

13. Dan felt **stumped** when Jenny's handwriting did not match the note. How did he feel?
    a. like the stump of a tree
    b. short
    c. like he did not know what was going on

Why Did It Happen?

◆ **Directions:** Draw a line from each event to the reason it happened.

What Happened	Why
14. Dan started to eat his lunch fast.	○ Dan wanted to get a look at Jenny's handwriting.
15. Dan walked by Jenny's desk.	○ Dan believed that it was Jenny who liked him.
16. Skye felt sad and mad.	○ Dan wanted to spy on the girls.
17. Dan sat by a plant to eat.	○ Dan wanted to get back to his locker by 12:20.

Look Ahead

◆ **18.** What will Dan do next? Write what you think on the lines below. Read on to find out.

_____

_____

Letters and Sounds

These words have the long **u** sound.

rule   school   blue

> ▶ **TIP:** The letter patterns **u**-consonant-**e**, **oo**, and **ue** all stand for the long **u** sound.

◆ **Directions:** Read these words. Circle the words that have the long **u** sound.

1. cool	4. flute	7. clue	10. tune
2. true	5. flux	8. soon	11. some
3. buck	6. shoot	9. stuck	

◆ **Directions:** Write each word you circled under the word that has the same pattern of letters for long **u**.

rule	school	blue
12. _____	14. _____	17. _____
13. _____	15. _____	18. _____
	16. _____	

◆ **Directions:** Write the letters on the lines. See how many words you can make.

sh	p	b	t	c	st	h	dr

19. _____ oot   23. _____ ool

20. _____ oot   24. _____ ool

21. _____ oot   25. _____ ool

22. _____ oot   26. _____ ool

Story Words

Word Bank

Write each of these story words in the Word Bank at the back of this book.

 **Directions:** Read each word to yourself. Then say the word out loud. Write the word on the line. Check the box after each step.

27. different   Read ❑ Say ❑ Write ❑ _____
      (dif | fer | ent)

28. should   Read ❑ Say ❑ Write ❑ _____

29. old   Read ❑ Say ❑ Write ❑ _____

30. tonight (to | night)   Read ❑ Say ❑ Write ❑ _____

31. dance   Read ❑ Say ❑ Write ❑ _____

More Word Work

> **TIP:** When you come to a longer word, look for smaller parts that make it up.
>
> ▸ Is it made up of a word and an ending?
>
> ▸ Is it made up of two smaller words?
>
> Find the smaller parts you know. Then read the whole word.

 **Directions:** Read each word below. Then write the smaller parts that make it up.

Examples: sailboat   =   sail + boat
           snugly   =   snug + ly
           guppies   =   guppy + es
           differently = different + ly

32. basketball   =   _____ + _____

33. lightly   =   _____ + _____

34. questioning =   _____ + _____

35. surprises   =   _____ + _____

36. serving   =   _____ + _____

37. pointed   =   _____ + _____

38. handmade   =   _____ + _____

39. hamburger   =   _____ + _____

OUT OF SIGHT

Dan still sat out of sight, hidden by the plants. He did not know what to do. At first he thought Jenny had been the one writing him notes. He thought Jenny liked him. He liked the idea of getting to know Jenny. Then he found out different. Skye was the writer of the letters. This changed the picture. Dan did not have a clue as to what he should do.

Studying Skye's sad face, Dan felt sad for her. "There is only one right thing to do, old boy," he thought. He got up and walked around the plants. He went right up to Skye and Jenny. Jenny looked up at him, while Skye looked like she wanted to run away. He said to Jenny, "Say, Jenny! It seems as if you like to pass notes for others, kind of like a letter service. Did you give my note to the shy Miss Skye?"

Jenny looked at Dan with a small smile. Skye just looked shocked. "As a matter of fact," she cried, "I was about to give it to her!" She passed Dan's note over to Skye.

"Skye," said Dan, "I have a question for you. You do not have to answer right now. But you will have to answer soon. Will you go out with me? Will you go to the Blue Moon dance with me, tonight?" Skye sat there. She was looking down at her lap, thinking about what she should do. Waiting for Skye to answer, Dan found himself catching Jenny's look again. She smiled brightly, giving him a nod and a wink.

Dan thought, "Jenny, you are so cute. And what a good friend you are to Skye." But he did not say anything.

What do you think will happen? Will Skye go out with Dan?

Circle your answer.　　　　　YES　　　　NO

Then keep reading to find out what happens next.

At last, Skye looked up. "OK, Dan. I will go with you to the dance. I will meet you there at 8:00."

Dan left his house at 7:45. He was waiting in the light rain at the school by 8:00. Soon Skye's mother drove up the road and dropped off the girls. Skye had on old faded blue jeans, a blue tank top, and black boots. Jenny wore black pants and a different kind of top with a spray of black rosebuds painted on it. The girls looked like a million bucks!

Dan walked with Skye and Jenny into the dance hall. Jenny and Dan chatted. Skye did not say much. "Maybe she is still feeling shy," Dan thought.

Inside, it was hard to talk. The DJ had the speakers turned way up. The lights were turned way down. "There's Calvin! Calvin! Over here!" hooted Jenny at a tall boy who was looking over at the three of them. "How cool! I am going to dance with Calvin. See you two after a while." Jenny ran over to Calvin, and soon they were dancing.

Dan grabbed Skye's hand and led her out to dance. Skye moved stiffly, as if she felt strange being with him. Dan tried to talk with her, but she did not look at him much. Dan felt foolish. "I thought she liked me," he thought. "Tonight it is hard to tell." Dan kept trying. After two more dances, it was the same old thing. Skye said, "I am going to get some food." She walked away fast.

Dan waited at the side of the room. Skye was away for a long while. "I do not get this," thought Dan. "Skye is out of sight again. That name is a true fit for her. Where is she?" Just as he was thinking he should go find her, he spotted her. She was dancing with Calvin! And she was smiling and talking. Now that was something different!

"Dan! Looks like Calvin and Skye are having fun!" Jenny was right next to him, yelling. Dan turned to look at Jenny. Her bright face was all lit up. He looked back over at Skye and Calvin. Then he looked back at Jenny and made his face droop in a goofy way. "I thought she liked me, but she seems to be having more fun with Calvin," he yelled back. "With me, she is like her code name: Out of Sight."

Jenny looked up at him, smiling. "You know, Dan, I like you. I like talking—I mean, yelling—with you!"

Dan smiled back at her. "I like you, too, Jenny. And I am glad you are not Out of Sight, because I cannot wait to dance with you tonight!"

What Do You Think?

◆ 1. Did things work out well for Dan, Skye, and Jenny? Why do you think as you do?

_____

_____

_____

Think About the Story

Use Story Words

◆ **Directions:** Look at your list of story words on page 151. Write a story word on each line.

2. fun way to move _____

3. means "not the same" _____

4. this night _____

5. one who has lived a long time _____

6. could have, would have, __?__ have _____

The Big Idea

◆ 7. Which sentence best sums up the end of the story? Circle the sentence.

    a. Dan finds out that he and Jenny like each other.

    b. Skye gets a boyfriend named Calvin.

    c. Five friends go to a dance and have a great time.

When Did It Happen?

◆ 8. Write a number from 1 to 6 in front of each event to show when it happened.

_____ Skye, Dan, and Jenny get to the dance.

_____ Dan asks Jenny if she gave the note to Skye.

_____ Skye dances with Dan.

_____ Jenny and Dan say they like each other.

_____ Dan asks Skye to go out with him.

_____ Jenny dances with Calvin.

Write Sentences About the Story

Directions: Use words from the story to answer these questions.

9. Dan said Jenny is running "a kind of letter service." Why did he say this?

_____

_____

10. How did Dan know that Skye had had a change of feelings and did not really like him any more?

_____

_____

11. Who likes whom at the end of the story?

Why Did It Happen?

Directions: Draw a line from each event to the reason it happened.

What Happened	Why
12. Dan did not have a clue about what to do.	○ Jenny smiled and winked.
13. Dan thought, "Jenny, you are so cute."	○ Skye felt strange being with Dan.
14. Skye walked away from Dan at the dance.	○ Calvin and Skye were dancing.
15. Jenny and Dan started having fun together.	○ Dan thought Jenny liked him and then found out it was Skye who liked him.

Letters and Sounds

Read these sentences.

▶ I **will not** see my girlfriend tonight.

▶ I **won't** see my girlfriend tonight.

◀▶ **1.** Which word in the second sentence takes the place of two words in the first sentence? _____

2. What words in the first sentence were replaced?

_____ and _____

▲ **TIP:** ▶ Sometimes you can put two words together to make one word called a **contraction**.

▲ ▶ A contraction is shorter than the two words that make it up.

▲ ▶ In a contraction, one or more letters are dropped. This mark takes their place: **'**

▲ ▶ The words **will** and **not** are often used in contractions.

◀▶ **Directions:** Read these words. Draw a line to match each contraction with the words that make it up.

3. won't ○ cannot

4. don't ○ did not

5. can't ○ is not

6. didn't ○ are not

7. isn't ○ will not

8. aren't ○ do not

◀▶ **Directions:** Read these words. Draw a line from each contraction to the words that make it up.

9. I'll ○ you will

10. you'll ○ he will

11. he'll ○ they will

12. she'll ○ I will

13. they'll ○ we will

14. we'll ○ she will

Story Words

Word Bank

Write each of these story words in the Word Bank at the back of this book.

◆ **Directions:** Read each word to yourself. Then say the word out loud. Write the word on the line. Check the box after each step.

15. ski   Read ❑ Say ❑ Write ❑ _____

16. patrol (pa│trol)   Read ❑ Say ❑ Write ❑ _____

17. snow   Read ❑ Say ❑ Write ❑ _____

18. board   Read ❑ Say ❑ Write ❑ _____

19. trouble (trou│ble)   Read ❑ Say ❑ Write ❑ _____

More Word Work

◆ **Directions:** Write these words again. Make them into contractions.

Example: is not = isn't

Contractions with *not*	Contractions with *will*
20. did not = _____	25. I will = _____
21. do not = _____	26. you will = _____
22. will not = _____	27. he will = _____
23. have not = _____	28. they will = _____
24. does not = _____	29. she will = _____

◆ **Directions:** Write each sentence again. Make the **bold** words into contractions.

30. I **do not** know how to ski.

_____

31. Jack **does not** have skis or boots.

_____

32. **He will** rent them at the ski shop.

_____

33. Snowboarding **is not** for me.

_____

34. I hope **you will** meet us at the slopes!

_____

SNOW JOB

Jan and Val waited in the chilly air at the top of the hill for their boss, Marie. They had their snowboards with them. They zipped up their coats and set their masks over their faces. It was the twins' first training shift as trail workers for the ski patrol. They were learning how to set up the hill for night use. Marie, on skis, got off the **lift** and pushed over to the twins. They looked down the slope in the fading daylight.

"This main run will be open tonight," said Marie. "See, it is well lit. We'll close off the trails to the sides, the tree runs, because they'll be in the dark. They aren't open at night at all. It is far too risky to let people ride or ski through the trees in the dark. I'll show you how to rig up the **markers** and ropes to close that first side trail to the right, over there. Then you two can close the other side trails. After that, check with me at the base. By then, I may have some patrol sleds for you to take back up to the top. OK, meet you at that first trail."

Marie pushed off, making swift, smooth turns down the hill. Not waiting, Jan started in right after her down the run, carving S-shaped turns down to where Marie had stopped. Val followed, smoothly changing from one edge of her board to the other through the turns. The snow under the edges of the board made a crunchy sound as it started to freeze up in the night air.

The three of them worked quickly to set up the ropes and safety markers to block off the top of the trail. Marie studied the snow on the main run. "That steep left side of the main trail is fast turning into an ice sheet," she said. "Why don't you rope it off right now? Then take a run down to the patrol shack to get more rope and markers. Then close off the rest of the side trails. Remember, stay out of the trees after dark! Now you work for the ski patrol. People look up to you. If you tell someone to stay off a trail, and then you go on it, it doesn't look good."

"But I thought ski patrol workers can ride where they want to!" said Jan. "Can't we go where we want to? We are great snowboarders. We'll be safe."

"It is true that ski patrol workers can go into closed areas when needed," said Marie. "You can only go to help someone in trouble, to check the trails, or to open and close them."

"OK, OK," said Val. "We get the picture."

"All right. I'll see you at the patrol base when you get down there." With that, Marie pointed her skis downhill and swooped off through the night mist.

Jan grinned and lobbed a question at Val. "Are you thinking what I am thinking?" she said. "Marie said we could go and check the trails, didn't she? Why don't we take a quick run through the trees and check the trails there! I haven't been through there at night. Then we can catch the short lift and ride back up to close the ice patch."

What do you think will happen next? Will Jan and Val go through the trees? Circle your answer.

YES   NO

Then keep reading to find out what they do.

Jan didn't need to talk Val into it. Val was set to go. She said, "Great idea. Marie did say we could go on the trail to check it or close it. We'll do that—check it and then close it!"

"What are we waiting for?" Jan cried out. "Come on!"

Jan and Val turned off the main trail and dodged through the trees. They whizzed fast, taking different paths back and forth in the dark. Jan fell one time when a small animal ran by, but she wasn't going fast, and she was OK. Coming out of the trees, they stopped. Val said, "OK, those trails need to be closed. Don't you think?"

"You bet!" yelled Jan as she pushed off again into the open, lighted area. The twins sped down the hill to catch the lift back to the top. ▶

You Be the Judge

◀▶ **1.** Do you think Val and Jan are the right people for this job? Why or why not? Write what you think on the lines below.

_____

_____

_____

Think About the Story

Use Story Words

◀▶ **Directions:** Look at your list of story words on page 157. Write a story word on each line.

2. I am long, flat, and hard. I am a _____.

3. I am made of frozen water. I am _____.

4. Our job is to keep people safe. We are a _____.

5. I speed down a snowy hill. I _____.

6. People are never glad to see me. I am _____.

What Are the Facts?

◀▶ **Directions:** Write **T** by the sentences that tell about the ski area. Write **F** by the sentences that do not.

7. _____ It has a lot of hills.

8. _____ It is not open at night.

9. _____ It has some areas that are closed.

10. _____ People must hike to the top of the runs.

11. _____ The ski area is for skiers only.

When Did It Happen?

◀▶ **12.** Write a number from 1 to 5 in front of each event to show when it happened.

_____ Jan, Val, and Marie work quickly to set up ropes and markers.

_____ Jan asks, "Are you thinking what I am thinking?"

_____ Jan and Val catch a lift back to the top.

_____ Jan and Val wait for their boss.

_____ Jan and Val go snowboarding in a closed area.

Write Sentences About the Story

◆ **Directions:** Use words from the story to answer these questions.

13. Where are Val and Jan working?

_____

14. When can ski patrol workers go into closed areas?

_____

_____

15. Are the twins following the rules? Why or why not?

_____

_____

Words and Meanings

◆ **Directions:** Think about how the **bold** words are used in the story. Then circle the words that show the meaning of each word or phrase.

16. In this story, a **lift** is _____.
   a. a ride up a hill at a ski area
   b. a kind of ski run
   c. a ride in a friend's car

17. In this story, what are **markers** used for?
   a. They are used to make pictures.
   b. They are used to make dark lines in the snow.
   c. They are used to show areas that are closed to skiers.

18. Jan yells, **"You bet!"** She means _____.
   a. "I'll bet you five bucks."
   b. "Yes!"
   c. "You bet, and you lost."

Look Ahead

◆ **19.** Do you think Val and Jan will start to do their job right? What might happen to change the way they see their work? Write what you think on the lines below. Then read on to see if you are right.

_____

_____

_____

Letters and Sounds

◆ **Directions:** Read these sentences.

▶ **He is** gliding down the slope.

▶ **He's** gliding down the slope.

1. Which word in the second sentence takes the place of two words

   in the first sentence? _____

2. What words in the first sentence were replaced?

   _____ and _____

△ **TIP:** ▶ You know that you can put two words together to make one
   word called a **contraction.** In a contraction, one or more
△   letters are dropped. This mark takes their place: **'**

△   ▶ The words **is** and **are** are often used in contractions.

◆ **Directions:** Read these words. Draw a line to match each contraction
with the two words that make it up.

3. he's   ○ what is

4. she's   ○ Jim is

5. it's   ○ he is

6. what's   ○ it is

7. Jim's   ○ she is

◆ **Directions:** Read these words. Draw a line from each contraction to
the words that make it up.

8. they're   ○ we are

9. we're   ○ you are

10. you're   ○ they are

△ **REMEMBER:** ▶ Use **is** with **he, she,** and **it.**

△   ▶ Use **are** with **we, you,** and **they.**

Story Words

◆ **Directions:** Read each word to yourself. Then say the word out loud. Write the word on the line. Check the box after each step.

11. America   Read ❑ Say ❑ Write ❑ _____
      (A | mer | i | ca)

12. world   Read ❑ Say ❑ Write ❑ _____

13. radio   Read ❑ Say ❑ Write ❑ _____

More Word Work

◆ **Directions:** Write each set of two words again. Make them into a contraction.

Example: what is = what's

Contractions with *is*	Contractions with *are*
14. he is = _____	17. they are = _____
15. she is = _____	18. you are = _____
16. it is = _____	19. we are = _____

◆ **Directions:** Write each sentence again. Make the **bold** words into contractions.

20. I **do not** have any cash.

_____

21. **We are** going to the bank.

_____

22. **Joe is** coming with us.

_____

23. **He will** bring his ATM card.

_____

24. **That will** solve our problem.

_____

25. **It is** great to have an ATM card.

_____

SNOW TROUBLE

Jan and Val had been on the job for three nights at Snow America. It was more like play than work. The whole picture was great: brisk air, huge night sky high over the treetops, and endless trails—and the fun of snowboarding all the time. It was great. They also snuck in some runs again each night on closed trails.

Then it snowed. When Jan and Val came to work, snow was still being dumped from the sky. The whole hill was deep in new snow, with more coming down. Their job got harder. This was because they had to dig ropes and markers out of the deep snow. Not only that, but a big snowboard race was coming up on the weekend. The girls had to work hard digging to keep the jumps and turns in shape on the race trail. Even so, they were thrilled. World-class snowboarders from all over America were coming to their hill—to Snow America. Also, it seemed like a world of people from all over America had come for the race. Night was falling and the air was getting chilly fast. But the slopes were still thick with snowboard riders.

"It's different with this snow," chattered Jan with a shiver. She yanked the hood of her coat over her hat. "I'm frozen stiff. Tonight is the hardest work yet." The snow was falling fast and thick. The ski patrol felt that the upper parts of the hill should be closed. Marie asked the twins to ride up to the top and **sweep the runs**. They were to ask people to leave the trails and then close off those trails. Then they were to check that no one was left on the hill.

They rode down the main run. The lights were on, but it was very hard to see through the thick falling snow. The side trails were closed and dark. They thought they were just about through with this trail. All of a sudden, a snowboarder sailed past them at top speed. "Hey, put the brakes on, dude!" yelled Val. "He could have hit us! He's going way too fast. Now there's a true fool who's going to end up in trouble!" she said to Jan.

Just then, the snowboarder missed making a turn. He was at the edge of the trail. Jan and Val squinted through the falling snow. They thought he went off the trail and into the trees. "What's he doing?" cried Jan. "He's in the trees. Doesn't he know that part of the hill is closed? Come on, Val. He may be in trouble."

What do you think happened to the snowboarder? Is he in trouble? Circle your answer.

YES   NO

Then read on to find out if you are right.

Jan and Val went to the area where they saw the snowboarder slip away from the main run. They looked off the trail into the dark.

"We have to go through the trees," said Val. "We have to find that rider."

"I don't know, Val," said Jan. "It's hard to see. Maybe he got through the trees fine."

"Well, we can't just leave. He might be in there."

Just then a shrill cry came from the tree area. "I think he's in trouble," said Val. She opened up her chest pack to find her radio. She said to Jan, "I think we better call for help." Val turned on the radio and called the ski patrol base.

Soon Marie and two other ski patrol members got there. They had a sled with them. Marie led the way into the trees. They shone their flashlights through the dark, this way and that. Then they spotted him. It looked as if he had hit the tree hard. His board had come off his boots and was away to one side. He was lying very still in the snow, and his leg was bleeding. Marie started to talk to him, but he was having trouble talking. He did not seem to know what happened. Marie had the base team radio for a rescue truck. They strapped him onto a **backboard** and placed him on the sled. Then they made their way, a bit at a time, out of the trees.

Jan and Val hung back. They looked on to see what the ski patrollers were doing, but they didn't go too close. They didn't say a thing. They were feeling bad. It was the first time they had seen anyone knocked out on the slopes. Jan looked over at Val. She could read Val's thoughts.

"I know you are thinking about how we went in the trees when we shouldn't have," Jan said. "Now I see why some trails are closed."

"I think it wasn't real to me that people can get really harmed out here," said Val. "Snowboarding and this job just seemed like so much fun. Like this snowboarder, I just wasn't thinking. Up to now, we've been lucky. Maybe we should start being smart."

You Be the Judge

◆ 1. What do you think the twins learned from seeing the snowboarder wipe out? Do you think they will do their job differently now? How? Write what you think on the lines below.

_____

_____

_____

Think About the Story

Use Story Words

◆ **Directions:** Look at your list of story words on page 163. Write a story word on each line.

2. the land we live in _____

3. tunes come out of this _____

4. all there is _____

Write Sentences About the Story

◆ **Directions:** Use words from the story to answer these questions.

5. Why did Jan and Val's jobs seem like all fun to them at first?

_____

_____

6. What changed the way they thought about their job?

_____

_____

7. Why did the girls feel bad at the end of the story?

_____

_____

8. Why did the snowboarder get into trouble?

_____

_____

When Did It Happen?

◆ **9.** Write a number from 1 to 6 by each event to show when it happened.

_____ Marie asked the twins to sweep the top runs.

_____ A snowboarder flew past the twins and off the trail.

_____ A big snow fell on Snow America.

_____ The rescue truck went to save the snowboarder.

_____ Val called Marie on her radio.

_____ The job at Snow America just seemed like fun.

Words and Meanings

◆ **Directions:** Think about how the **bold** words are used in the story. Then circle the words that show the meaning of each word or phrase.

10. To **sweep the runs** means to _____.

    a. clean the runs with a broom

    b. get all the people off the runs

    c. close the runs before people get to them

11. In this story, a **backboard** is _____.

    a. a long, flat board used for rescue

    b. the back part of a basketball hoop

    c. a kind of snowboard used for tricks.

What Are the Facts?

◆ **Directions:** Put a **T** next to the sentences that tell about Snow America. Put an **F** next to the sentences that do not.

12. _____ It doesn't snow that hard there.

13. _____ Sometimes at night the hills are filled with snowboarders.

14. _____ If you get lost there, no one will rescue you.

15. _____ World-class snowboarders sometimes go there.

16. _____ A rescue can't take place at night.

Letters and Sounds

◆ **Directions:** Read these sentences.

▶ **We had** gone to the mall.

▶ **We'd** gone to the mall.

1. Which word in the second sentence takes the place of two words in the first sentence? _____

2. What words in the first sentence were replaced?

_____ and _____

▲
▲ **TIP:** ▶ You know that sometimes you can put two words together
▲   to make one word called a **contraction**.

▶ The words **had, have,** and **has** are often used in
   contractions.

◆ **Directions:** Read these words. Draw a line to match each
   contraction with the words that make it up.

3. I'd   ○ she had

4. you'd   ○ they had

5. he'd   ○ he had

6. she'd   ○ we had

7. we'd   ○ I had

8. they'd   ○ you had

◆ **Directions:** Read these words. Draw a line from each contraction to
   the words that make it up

9. I've   ○ she has

10. you've   ○ they have

11. we've   ○ we have

12. they've   ○ I have

13. she's   ○ he has

14. he's   ○ you have

Story Words

Word Bank

Write each of these story words in the Word Bank at the back of this book.

◆ **Directions:** Read each word to yourself. Then say the word out loud. Write the word on the line. Check the box after each step.

15. blind   Read ❑ Say ❑ Write ❑ _____

16. chair   Read ❑ Say ❑ Write ❑ _____

17. disabled (dis│a│bled) Read ❑ Say ❑ Write ❑ _____

18. disability   Read ❑ Say ❑ Write ❑ _____
    (dis│a│bil│i│ty)

19. outrigger   Read ❑ Say ❑ Write ❑ _____
    (out│rig│ger)

More Word Work

◆ **Directions:** Write these words again. Make them into contractions.

Example: is not = isn't

Contractions with *have* and *has*	Contractions with *had*
20. I have = _____	**25.** I had = _____
21. you have = _____	**26.** you had = _____
22. we have = _____	**27.** we had = _____
23. they have = _____	**28.** they had = _____
24. she has = _____	**29.** he had = _____

◆ **Directions:** Write each sentence again. Make the **bold** words into contractions.

30. **I have** seen snowboarders on the slopes.

_____

31. My **sister is** a teacher.

_____

32. **She is** teaching kids how to ski.

_____

33. **She has** been doing this for years.

_____

34. **It is** not easy to learn how to ski.

_____

Use What You Know

How can people with disabilities take part in sports? Write what you know on the lines. Then read on to find out about how skiers with disabilities can take part in snow sports.

_____

_____

_____

_____

_____

NO SUCH THING AS CAN'T

Picture this. You're skiing down a steep, snowy slope. All of a sudden you see a skier who has on a sign, "Blind Skier." Would you be shocked? Or maybe a great skier passes you who has only one leg. That would be different, wouldn't it? It's true—many people with disabilities now learn to ski, snowboard, and take part in many sports! For these people, there is no such word as "can't." They know they can.

In America, the Americans with Disabilities Act looks after people with disabilities. It says that public areas must serve people who have disabilities, as well as serving millions of others. Winter sports areas must also do this. Ski and snowboard training can be changed to fit the needs of people who have disabilities.

New kinds of tools

Sometimes people must invent new tools to teach a skier with a disability. These tools include poles, straps, chairs, crutches, and different kinds of boots. Long straps called tethers may be used to help a skier keep standing while moving. The teacher also uses tethers to help the skier make turns.

A tether helps blind skiers learn how to move on the snow. Soon, the blind skier may ski without the tether. Even then, a buddy stays close by the blind skier at all times. The buddy calls out what is coming up on the path. The buddy keeps talking to the blind skier. He or she tells the skier where trees, poles, and other people are. The buddy also calls out the turns. Some blind and one-legged skiers have the skill to go on even the highest, steepest slopes!

A skier hits the slopes.

Here are some other tools for skiers and snowboarders with disabilities:

▲ **Outriggers.** These are small skis fixed to the ends of crutches. A skier can then use one or two skis, plus two outriggers—one on each arm—to help with staying upright and making turns. People who have trouble standing up or who have only one leg may learn to ski this way.

▲ **Chair skis.** The chair ski may have one or two large skis fixed under it. It may also have two small outrigger skis, out to each side. If people can't move their legs, or if they're missing legs, they can sit in a chair ski. By leaning left or right, they learn to make turns.

"Everyone should know that I'm having a blast!" says Michael. Michael is a skier who cannot walk, but rides in a chair ski. "I don't think people should give up on life if they're disabled. I've taken something bad and turned it into something good! Now others can see me and know that they can do it, too!"

You Be the Judge

◆ 1. Why is the Americans with Disabilities Act important? Write what you think on the lines below.

_____

_____

_____

Think About the Story

Use Story Words

◆ **Directions:** Look at your list of story words on page 169. Write a story word on each line.

2. Having a _____ does not mean you can't take part in sports.

3. Many _____ people have learned to ski or to snowboard.

4. A _____ skier skis with a buddy who can see.

5. People without the use of their legs ski with the help of a _____.

6. An _____ is a small ski that fits on the end of a crutch.

Write Sentences About the Story

◆ **Directions:** Use words from the story to answer these questions.

7. How does a tether help a blind person learn to ski?

_____

_____

8. What does a buddy do for a blind skier?

_____

_____

9. What is the name of one tool used to help people with disabilities learn to ski? How is that tool used?

_____

_____

What Does It Do?

◆ **Directions:** Draw a line from each tool to the job it does.

10. tether   ◯ lets a skier who has no legs ski while sitting down

11. outrigger on a chair ski   ◯ helps a skier make turns while standing upright

12. chair ski   ◯ helps a blind skier keep standing and make turns

13. crutch with outrigger   ◯ helps a skier make turns while seated

Write About It

◆ **Directions:** Write a sentence about each tool. Use your answers from **What Does It Do?** to help you.

14. tether

_____

_____

15. outrigger on a chair ski

_____

_____

16. outrigger on a crutch

_____

_____

17. chair ski

_____

_____

What Do You Think?

◆ 18. The title of this story is "No Such Thing as **Can't.**" What do you think this title means?

_____

_____

Chapter 3: Summary of Skills and Strategies

Let's look back at what you learned in Chapter 3.

Letters and Sounds

◆ You learned . . .

  ▸ how to read words that start with three consonants.

  ▸ that lots of letter patterns can stand for the long **a, i, o,** and **u** vowel sounds.

Stories and Skills

◆ You learned . . .

  ▸ about characters who learned some big lessons on the job.

  ▸ about the different kinds of jobs teens do in America.

  ▸ how people with disabilities take part in snow sports.

◆ You learned . . .

  ▸ how to understand stories better by using what you know.

  ▸ how to predict what might happen next in a story.

Words and Meanings

◆ You learned . . .

  ▸ a lot of new words, including some long ones!

  ▸ that compound words are words made up of two smaller words put together.

  ▸ how to read and write contractions.

  ▸ that looking for smaller words or word parts can help you read longer words.

The chapter review will give you a chance to show what you have learned.

Part A

Summing It Up: Letters and Sounds

- ▸ Sometimes three consonants come together at the beginning of a word.
- ▸ In the blends **scr, str,** and **spr,** each letter stands for one sound. You can hear three sounds at the beginning of **scrap, strip,** and **spring.**
- ▸ The letters **squ** stand for this sound: **skw. Squ** stands for the sound at the beginning of the word **squirrel.**
- ▸ The letters in **shr** and **thr** stand for two sounds. You can hear two sounds at the beginning of **shrink** and **threw.**

Directions: Write each word in the list next to the sentence that tells about it.

squint	**throne**	**scrape**
spring	**shrink**	**squirrel**
throat	**streams**	**shrimp**

1. This little animal lives in the sea. _____

2. When it rains, these fill up. _____

3. This means "to get smaller." _____

4. This is the time of year when snow melts. _____

5. A queen or king sits here. _____

6. Your food goes down this when you eat. _____

7. You might do this in the sun. _____

8. This animal is small, cute, and fast. _____

9. This is a little rip in your skin. _____

> ▸ The letters **ai** can stand for the long **a** sound.
> ▸ The letter pattern **a**-consonant-**e** can stand for the long **a** sound.

Directions: Draw a line under each word that has the long **a** sound. Then circle the letters that stand for that sound.

10. stand	**12.** gale	**14.** faint	**16.** fade
11. stale	**13.** glad	**15.** fans	**17.** tram

> ▸ Many patterns of letters can stand for the long **i** sound.
> ▸ The letters **igh** and the letter **y** can stand for the long **i** sound.

Directions: Circle the words that have the long **i** sound.

18. pin	**20.** pine	**22.** my	**24.** might	**26.** shy
19. grime	**21.** high	**23.** fright	**25.** figs	**27.** sly

Directions: Write each word under the word that has the same pattern of letters for long **i**.

cry	sight	time
28. _____	**31.** _____	**34.** _____
29. _____	**32.** _____	**35.** _____
30. _____	**33.** _____	

> ▸ Many patterns of letters can stand for the long **o** sound.
> ▸ The letters **oa** can stand for the long **o** sound.
> ▸ The letter pattern **o**-consonant-**e** can stand for the long **o** sound.

Directions: Draw a line under the words that have the long **o** sound. Then circle the letters that stand for that sound.

36. tote	**38.** groan	**40.** bone	**42.** pole	**44.** tone
37. clock	**39.** moat	**41.** stock	**43.** goats	**45.** moan

176 *Chapter 3*

▸ Many patterns of letters can stand for the long **u** sound.
▸ The letter pattern **u**-consonant-**e** stands for the long **u** sound.
▸ The letters **oo** and **ue** can stand for the long **u** sound.

◆ **Directions:** Write each word under the word that has the same pattern of letters for long **u.**

tune	fool	blue	mute	root
cool	sue	spruce	clue	zoom

flute	pool	true
46. _____	49. _____	53. _____
47. _____	50. _____	54. _____
48. _____	51. _____	55. _____
	52. _____	

▸ You can put some words together to form a **contraction.**
▸ In a contraction, one or more letters are replaced with this mark: '
▸ The words **will, not, has, have, had, are,** and **is** are often used in contractions.

◆ **Directions:** Read each contraction. Write the two words that make it up.

Example: aren't = are + not

56. isn't   = _____ + _____

57. you'll   = _____ + _____

58. haven't = _____ + _____

59. I've   = _____ + _____

60. doesn't = _____ + _____

61. you're   = _____ + _____

Part B

Summing It Up: More Word Work

> ▸ Adding **e** to a word like **dim** or **can** gives the word a long vowel sound. Words like **dime** and **cane** have the CVCe pattern.
>
> ▸ Two vowels next to each other can also have a long vowel sound. **Mean, need,** and **main** are examples. These words have the CVVC pattern.

Directions: Write each word in the box where it belongs.

reach	choke	coats
mine	time	tries
boat	steed	slope

CVCe pattern	CVVC pattern
1. _____	5. _____
2. _____	6. _____
3. _____	7. _____
4. _____	8. _____
	9. _____

When you add **s** or **es** to a word that ends in **y,** change **y** to **i.** Then add the ending.

Directions: Add **es** to each word below. Write the new word on the line. Change **y** to **i.**

Example: cry + es = cries

10. try + es   = _____

11. fly + es   = _____

12. puppy + es = _____

13. spy + es   = _____

Some words are made up of two smaller words that have been put together. These are called **compound words.**

◆ **Directions:** Read each word. Write the two smaller words that make it up.

Example: highway = high + way

14. racetrack = _____ + _____

15. sandbox = _____ + _____

16. housefly = _____ + _____

17. benchmark = _____ + _____

18. popcorn = _____ + _____

When you come to a longer word, look for smaller parts that make it up.
 ▶ Is it made of a word and an ending?
 ▶ Is it made up of two smaller words?
Find the smaller parts you know. Then read the whole word.

◆ **Directions:** Read each word below. Then write the smaller parts that make it up.

Example: differently = different + ly

19. questioner = _____ + _____

20. basketball = _____ + _____

21. pitcher = _____ + _____

22. friendly = _____ + _____

23. highway = _____ + _____

24. servicing = _____ + _____

25. snowboard = _____ + _____

Part C

Story Words

Directions: On the lines below, write the word from the list that matches each clue.

animal	picture	different
house	again	should
mother	change	old

1. has lived a long time _____
2. not the same _____
3. good to put on a wall _____
4. dog, cat, rat, or mule _____
5. a place to live _____
6. a mom _____
7. become different _____
8. one more time _____
9. would, could, __?__ _____

Directions: On the lines below, write a word from the list to finish each sentence.

question	burger	dance
idea	study	counselor
letter	answer	million

10. I asked my dad a _____.
11. He gave me his _____, which was "no."
12. I will work as a camp _____ next summer.
13. I had a _____ and fries for lunch.
14. Dan's girlfriend wrote him a long _____.
15. Shawn likes to _____ at parties.
16. I wish I had a _____ bucks.
17. Jen needs to _____ her math if she wants to pass.
18. Kim has a great _____ for a story.

◆ **Directions:** Read each word. On the lines below, write a number to tell how many syllables it has.

19. outrigger _____   24. disabled _____

20. disability _____   25. light _____

21. service _____   26. trouble _____

22. serve _____   27. patrol _____

23. world _____   28. found _____

◆ **Directions:** On the lines below, write the word from the list that matches each clue.

| America | thought | tonight | food | blind |
| chair | radio | snow | ski | spray |

29. what's for dinner _____

30. what a hose can do _____

31. sports, tunes, traffic, ads _____

32. an icy sport _____

33. fluffy white stuff _____

34. can't see _____

35. a great land _____

36. a form of **think** _____

37. the night that will follow this day _____

38. something to sit in _____

Part D

What Kind of Story?

◆ **Directions:** Write **nonfiction** next to the stories that tell about real people or places. Write **fiction** next to the stories that were made up.

1. "Camp Counselor" _____

2. "Summer Jobs for Teens" _____

3. "Out of Sight" _____

4. "Snow Trouble" _____

5. "No Such Thing as *Can't*" _____

Who Did This?

◆ **Directions:** This list has the names of some people who were in the stories in Chapter 3. Write a name to answer each question.

Jenny	Jan	Marie	Val
Kevin	Dan	Mike Strong	Skye

6. Who found notes on his locker? _____

7. Who was a boss on a ski patrol? _____

8. Who liked a boy and then changed her mind? _____

9. Who was a counselor-in-training? _____

10. Who snuck onto closed snow trails? _____ and

_____

11. Who liked Dan in the end? _____

12. Who was a lead counselor? _____

Where Did It Happen?

◆ **Directions:** This is a list of some spots where the stories took place. Write each place name by the story it goes with.

a tent	a dance hall
a school	an ice patch
Snow America	Camp Spring Hill

13. "Camp Counselor"

_____

_____

14. "Out of Sight"

_____

_____

15. "Snow Trouble"

_____

_____

Chapter 1 Story Words

◆ **Directions:** Write the words from the Story Words section of each lesson.

LESSON 1   ▶ **The Dive Game**

_____

_____

_____

_____

_____

LESSON 2   ▶ **Dive Deep**

_____

_____

_____

LESSON 3   ▶ **A Place to Skate**

_____

_____

_____

_____

Chapter 1 Story Words, continued

LESSON 4 ▶ **The Skate Ramp**

_____

_____

_____

_____

_____

LESSON 5 ▶ **Skate Shop Job**

_____

_____

_____

_____

LESSON 6 ▶ **Race Track Dreams**

_____

_____

_____

_____

_____

Chapter 1 Story Words, continued

LESSON 7　▶ **The Pace Car**

_____

_____

_____

_____

_____

LESSON 8　▶ **Getting a Job**

_____

_____

_____

_____

_____

Chapter 2 Story Words

◆ **Directions:** Write the words from the Story Words
section of each lesson.

LESSON 1 ▶ **The Girl in the Desert, Part 1**

_____

_____

_____

_____

_____

_____

LESSON 2 ▶ **The Girl in the Desert, Part 2**

_____

_____

_____

_____

_____

LESSON 3 ▶ **Tales from the Desert**

_____

_____

_____

_____

_____